A must-read book for men…and those who love them.

—Jon Gordon
Best-Selling Author, *The Carpenter* and *Training Camp*

This is an important book. I'm an avid reader, but this one book is a game changer. I believe it will be a soul-stirring gift to men and its impact will be felt by their mothers, sisters, wives, and children, indeed the whole body of Christ. When God's sons reject the lies of the enemy and embrace their strength, purpose, and destiny, it will be felt by the church, the nation, and the world.

—Sheila Walsh
Author, *Praying Women*

When you pick up a book about biblical manhood, you want to know that the author walks the talk and has proved the concepts he writes about to be true in his own life. I can think of no finer example of this than Tim Clinton. In the many years I have known Tim, I have personally seen him model biblical manhood as he has loved his wife, Julie; raised his incredible children, Megan and Zach; and worked tirelessly to lead thousands of men to the cross. I could not be more excited that he is now sharing his wisdom with other men through this book.

—Joe White
President, Kanakuk Ministries
Author and Speaker

Dr. Clinton is calling men to their true identity. He reminds us that in an age when culture tells us to seek our own ease and comfort, God calls us to something altogether different. Tim is telling all who will hear that their lives are much greater than themselves. After a lifetime of leadership and educating, Tim has amazing insight into human nature and the decisions we make. Tim has written an exceptional reminder to us all that God calls us to rise above our culture and be men He is proud to call His sons.

—Ken Harrison
Chairman and CEO, Promise Keepers

Dr. Tim Clinton and Max Davis have written a must-read book that will be discussed for years to come! I applaud them tackling a thorny topic in a thoughtful and biblical way.

—Dr. Robert Jeffress
Senior Pastor, First Baptist Church, Dallas
Author, *Courageous*

Men have reached a pivotal moment in history and now stand at a crossroads. Will they let culture define what masculinity is…or finally take back their voice and be strong for the sake of the next generation? *Take It Back* shows them the way!

—Josh D. McDowell
Author

I am a comedian. But the most serious job I have on this earth is being a mom to my son. Dr. Clinton has written an incredible book not only to guide my son but to strengthen my resolve for us both to become *all* God intended for us to be.

—Chonda Pierce
Author, Actress, Comedian, Mom

The meaning of a man has been lost in our generation. While culture is attempting to redefine manhood, it is time to return to the Bible to see what God says about what it means to be a man. This is why I am thankful for the call to every man that is issued by Dr. Tim Clinton and Max Davis in their book, *Take It Back*. From the inside out each man needs to step into this moment in history and step up to this dynamic challenge. Now is the time to carry out these words: "Be strong, and…be a man" (1 Kings 2:2, MEV).

—Dr. Ronnie Floyd
President and CEO, Southern Baptist Convention
Executive Committee

Men today are drowning in a sea of low expectations, where compromise wins over convictions and convenience replaces courage. Spiritual morality is redefined daily as many men sit on the sidelines of life, choosing to be entertained rather than challenged. In the midst of society's deafening noise, Dr. Tim Clinton draws the proverbial line in the sand and boldly declares, "Enough is enough!" Through the profound practicality of this book Clinton shouts a clarion call to all men: "Make your life count for God and His kingdom! Exhaust your gifts and die empty!"

Men, this book will not let you off the hook. In fact, chapter 17 alone—"A Regular Joe"—makes this a worthy read. It doesn't get any more regular than a shepherd boy or cupbearer! God is calling us to be restored to our rightful place as leaders, protectors, gatekeepers, and difference makers. Let's become a generation of men fully committed to one proposition: we are strategically here right now...to *take it back*!

—RICK RIGSBY, PHD
PRESIDENT, RICK RIGSBY COMMUNICATIONS
MOTIVATIONAL SPEAKER, CORPORATE COACH, MINISTER
BEST-SELLING AUTHOR, *LESSONS FROM A THIRD GRADE DROPOUT*

Take It Back ignites our duty as men. I know the author pretty well, and I can promise you that he lives out what he preaches and teaches. His presence and influence in my life help me every day to be the best version of myself and a man after God's own heart. I believe *Take It Back* will make you a stronger man who will be better equipped to live out and take back what God has for your life.

—ZACH CLINTON
COHOST, IGNITE MEN'S IMPACT WEEKEND

For too long men have believed the lies of the enemy! *Take It Back* is packed full of help, hope, and encouragement for men to take back their God-given responsibilities to impact the church, the home, and the culture for Christ.

—DR. TONY EVANS
PRESIDENT, THE URBAN ALTERNATIVE
SENIOR PASTOR, OAK CLIFF BIBLE FELLOWSHIP

This book has the power to change a generation! *Take It Back* encourages and emboldens men in a way that calls them to rise to the challenge of biblical manhood and lead their families and communities like Jesus.

—MARK BATTERSON
NEW YORK TIMES BEST-SELLING AUTHOR, *THE CIRCLE MAKER*
LEAD PASTOR, NATIONAL COMMUNITY CHURCH

It's been said, "If you preach to hurting people, you will never lack for an audience." Dr. Tim Clinton has that heart and reaches thousands every year through his writings and events. I am confident that Dr. Clinton and Max Davis' new book, *Take It Back: Reclaiming Biblical Manhood for the Sake of Marriage, Family, and Culture*, will help so many at this critical time in our nation's history. It's time for men to rise up and take their rightful place for the sake of marriage, family, and righteousness in the culture. *Take It Back* is sure to encourage, challenge, and inspire men for such a time as this.

—GREG LAURIE
PASTOR AND EVANGELIST, HARVEST MINISTRIES

Never before has it been more important to understand what it means to be a man created in God's image. Reclaiming God's design for manhood is vital for the health of our families, our relationships, and our nation. In *Take It Back*, Clinton and Davis clearly explain the biblical definition of *masculinity*, offer men practical advice on how they can follow God's call, and share encouraging stories of godly men who have influenced their cultures throughout history. This book is a must-read for every man in America.

—SAMUEL RODRIGUEZ
PRESIDENT, NATIONAL HISPANIC CHRISTIAN LEADERSHIP CONFERENCE
AUTHOR AND SPEAKER

Any man who writes about traditional masculinity today is bold. Tim Clinton and Max Davis have stepped up to the plate, and I believe every man who reads this book will be challenged—and changed. "The great need of our culture today," the authors write, "is not for more men of talent…but for more men of character with hearts that follow hard after God." Amen. May God use this message to help men take back their lives and then reclaim the culture, fulfilling God's kingdom purpose.

—JAMES ROBISON
FOUNDER AND PRESIDENT, LIFE OUTREACH INTERNATIONAL

There is simply no more-important subject than the subject of my friend Tim Clinton's book. The battle for biblical manhood is a battle to which we are all called. I thank God for Tim Clinton and this important book.

—ERIC METAXAS
AUTHOR, *BONHOEFFER: PASTOR, MARTYR, PROPHET, SPY*
HOST, *THE ERIC METAXAS SHOW*

Of the dozens of books on what it means to be a Christian man in the twenty-first century, none is as timely and relevant to life today as *Take It Back*, by Tim Clinton and Max Davis. This book doesn't miss a trick or a deception of the enemy that is common to the life of every man while arming you with the tools to overcome the temptations we all face. You really can become the man God is calling you to be, and each chapter is filled with very practical tools to help you find your way. This is a must-read for every man who seeks to follow Jesus with his whole heart.

—JENTEZEN FRANKLIN
SENIOR PASTOR, FREE CHAPEL
NEW YORK TIMES BEST-SELLING AUTHOR

Tim Clinton gets it. He is a man who knows what it takes to live, love, and lead well and impact the family God's way. He is both a prophet and a counselor, which is a great combination if you want to influence men and those who love them. *Take It Back* is a manifesto for men who want to change the world.

—JACK GRAHAM
PASTOR, PRESTONWOOD BAPTIST CHURCH
HEAD OF POWERPOINT MINISTRIES

The message in Dr. Tim Clinton and Max Davis' book, *Take It Back*, is backed up with solid biblical truth of how God wants men to be men. As you read, my hope is that you will be encouraged, challenged, and inspired to claim your true identity as a man.

—Robert Morris
Founding Lead Senior Pastor, Gateway Church
Best-Selling Author, *The Blessed Life, Beyond Blessed,* and
Take the Day Off

TAKE IT BACK

DR. TIM CLINTON
and MAX DAVIS

CHARISMA
HOUSE

Visit the author's websites at www.TimClinton.com and AACC.net.

Library of Congress Cataloging-in-Publication Data:

An application to register this book for cataloging has been submitted to the Library of Congress.

International Standard Book Number: 978-1-62999-875-6
E-book ISBN: 978-1-62999-876-3

21 22 23 24 25 — 9 8 7 6 5 4 3 2 1
Printed in the United States of America

To the men in the arena who are stepping up,
daring to be who God created them to be

I am about to go the way of all the earth. Be strong, and show yourself a man.

—1 Kings 2:2

Contents

Go ahead, make my day.
—HARRY CALLAHAN, *SUDDEN IMPACT*

Every man dies. Not every man really lives.
—WILLIAM WALLACE, *BRAVEHEART*

This time the mission is a man.
—SERGEANT HORVATH, *SAVING PRIVATE RYAN*

I'll be back.
—THE TERMINATOR, *THE TERMINATOR*

Aim small, miss small.
—BENJAMIN MARTIN, *THE PATRIOT*

It ain't about how hard you hit It's about how hard you can
get hit and keep moving forward.
—ROCKY BALBOA, *ROCKY BALBOA*

I have found David son of Jesse, *a man after my own heart*;
he will do everything I want him to do.[1]
—GOD, THE BIBLE

It is not the critic who counts; not the man who points out how the strong man stumbles or where the doer of deeds could have done them better. The credit belongs to the man who is actually in the arena, whose face is marred by dust and sweat and blood; who strives valiantly; who errs, who comes short again and again, because there is no effort without error and shortcoming; but who does actually strive to do the deeds; who knows the great enthusiasms, the great devotions; who spends himself in a worthy cause; who at the best knows in the end the triumph of high achievement, and who at the worst, if he fails, at least fails while daring greatly, so that his place shall never be with those cold and timid souls who neither know victory nor defeat.

—THEODORE ROOSEVELT, "CITIZENSHIP IN A REPUBLIC"

Foreword

I WAS NEVER TAUGHT how to be a man. To many my success on the field may have looked like the ultimate achievement for manhood, but deep down I was broken, searching, confused, and addicted. Growing up, my childhood was really tough—in part because of an abusive, alcoholic father who took out his anger on our family, especially my brother and me.

For years the words of my father haunted me: "You're never going to be anything. You don't get anything right." The lies that my father spoke over me became thoughts I believed about myself. Eventually my father walked out on us. I never had a father figure in my life to help me walk through the right doors, so I ended up walking through all of the wrong ones.

Playing for seventeen years, making eight consecutive All-Star Game appearances, and winning four World Series Championship titles, I was at the top of my game on the field but losing myself to the world of alcohol and drugs. Two broken marriages, the death of my mother, battling off and on with addiction, and colon cancer brought me to my knees and sent me into a deeper spiral. See, it wasn't until I came to the end of myself and my circumstances and fully surrendered to Jesus that everything changed for me as a man. I found my purpose in God. The lies I believed for a majority of my life that led me down the broken road of addiction were defeated by the truth of God's Word. And my views on what defined me as a man started to shift to the things God desires for manhood. What's burning inside of me now is a love for Jesus and helping the hurting of our society, especially men. Because I was hurting once upon a time, I don't want others to experience the same pain and chaos I did.

All of our stories are different, but there are two things that all men can do as we begin our journey to reclaim manhood. I believe in order to step into true biblical manhood, we must first come to the end of ourselves. Galatians 2:20 says, "I have been crucified with Christ and I no longer live, but Christ lives in me. The life I now live in the body, I live by faith in the Son of God, who loved me and gave himself for me" (NIV). As you read *Take It Back*, there will be things that God calls you to lay down; the biggest one will be yourself. As men we need to come to the end of ourselves in order to live out our God-given potential to influence our families, the culture, and the church.

The second thing we must do to step into biblical manhood is be forward-thinking, future-minded about the next generation, leaving a kingdom-impacting legacy. We have to wake up and realize that if we don't start teaching our sons real biblical principles, they're going to choose the wrong roads and buy into the lies of the enemy, surrendering biblical manhood to a culture that doesn't want men to thrive.

Take It Back is a call for men to rise up and live like Jesus and impact the culture in a way that will impact generations to come. This book is for men who have fallen prey to the attacks of culture. It is for men who have fallen down and need to get back up again. *Take It Back* shows men the way back to a relationship with God and those they love.

Men, we are at war. We're looking at spiritual brokenness in America. Everybody wants to put a bandage over it, but you can't put a bandage over the enemy. Because we have victory in Christ, victory is ours for the taking. Men, it is time to step up to the plate and *take it back*.

—DARRYL STRAWBERRY
FORMER MAJOR LEAGUE BASEBALL PLAYER, AUTHOR

Acknowledgments

A SPECIAL THANK-YOU GOES to our friends at Charisma for believing in *Take It Back*. What an amazing team of leaders and influencers led by Stephen Strang and Marcos Perez—Lucy, Debbie, Margarita, Melissa, SueLee, and Nicole—you guys are the best.

We are indebted to Kyle Sutton and Garrett Hedrick for their diligence and commitment to excellence every step of the way through the development of the manuscript and promotion strategies.

Max and I talk often about the steadfast love of the Lord—filled with grace, mercy, and forgiveness. Without Him, our lives would be lost.

I am grateful to my dad, James E. Clinton, who is in heaven; my brother, James D. Clinton; my spiritual mentor and friend, Dr. Ron Hawkins; my son, Zach Clinton; my son-in-law, Ben Allison; my siblings and extended family; and our entire AACC board and team for their love and daily influence that continues to shape me into the man I am. I'm graced with the love of my life, Julie, who holds my hand every day, and the special love of my daughter, Megan, and our first granddaughter, Olivia. It's beyond words.

—DR. TIM CLINTON

W ORKING WITH TIM Clinton on this project has been an honor. The experience has grown me both as a man and a writer. I've gained a friend in the process. I want to say a special thanks to my amazing wife, Alanna, whose insight on this manuscript was priceless. Also, to my dad, James E. Davis, who's been a model of biblical manhood to me.

—MAX DAVIS

Introduction

LISTEN. SOMETHING IS happening. Something is stirring—something so significant we can't even wrap our minds around it. It's like a tsunami coming…among men. There's fire. There's energy. God is waking the hearts of men to do one thing, to step into this moment, for such a time as this.

It's no secret. There's been a beatdown on men, on anything that's masculine, on anything that smacks of testosterone—from the radical push to feminize men to changing the core nature of what it means to be masculine. But God made man for a purpose and a reason. This book unpacks what men have lost, how significant the fight we are engaged in is, and how to step by step take back what we've lost and what we've given away.

This is a book of help, hope, and deep encouragement. It's a book anchored in faith that calls men to be men. When King David was on his deathbed, passing the baton of leadership to his son Solomon, there are so many things he could have said. Yet he told his son, "Be strong, and show yourself a man."[1] You know why David told Solomon that? Because men matter more than you know. Masculinity is important. But what did David mean? What does it really mean to be a man? What does real, biblical masculinity look like? You may be surprised. It's certainly not how the culture has misrepresented it.

You need to know that you matter as a man. You need to know you are not alone. Men everywhere, from every walk of life, are crying out, "God, I want my life to count. I want to make a difference. I want to be all that You created me to be."

It may seem as though everything is lost and this is your darkest hour. But God loves to meet you in your brokenness. He loves to use those moments to send you fleeing back to Him for hope and strength. It's in those difficult moments that you find, as David and his band of men did when faced with devastation at Ziklag, that it's never too late to saddle up and take it back! If you are looking for a defining moment in your life, this is it. God is saying, "Listen to Me. It's time! It's time to saddle up and recover all!"

We are so excited about what God could do through this book, whether it's bringing a dad closer to his kids, spurring a man to love his wife the way Christ loved the church, or motivating a man to drive a stake in the ground and say, "From this day forward I'm going to give my life for Christ and follow His lead!" Think of what Jesus did with just twelve men—He changed the world. Think of what could happen if men stood up and banded together for Christ.

Of course we celebrate women and their contribution. We know how significant they are in influence and leadership. We in no way want this book to put a negative light on women—but make no mistake about it, this is a book about and for men.

The chapters are short, powerful, and easy to read. At the end of each chapter are Discussion Questions to encourage you to dig a little deeper, either by yourself or in a group; a Sword of the Word verse for you to memorize or discuss to help arm you for battle; and a Pray About It section to give you a place to start when you are talking to God about the issues raised in this book. There is also an appendix with helpful resources in the back of the book.

So, go ahead. Turn the page and get ready to take it back! We can change the world one man at a time.

CHAPTER 1

The Comeback

Why does a man long for a battle to fight? Because when we enter the story in Genesis, we step into a world at war. The lines have already been drawn. Evil is waiting to make its next move.

—JOHN ELDREDGE

A s soon as the opening bell rang, his opponent charged at him, delivering swift, glancing jabs, then backing away like an annoying insect. Some thirty pounds heavier, George Foreman stood unflinching, a mighty oak, swaying but refusing to give. Waiting for his best shot, he didn't want to knock down the reigning heavyweight champion, Michael Moorer, too early. George knew that unless it was a knockout punch, Moorer would just bounce back up and then box from a distance, collecting points with those irritating jabs. To win, Foreman needed his opponent up close and personal so he could wear him down. Then, at the right time, he would land the punch that would keep him down. He just needed to be patient.

When Moorer threw a combination, Foreman carefully and meticulously countered with a jab of his own, making sure it connected. Although his adversary was throwing more punches, Foreman's punches were carrying more weight. Yet Moorer continued to land shots, some dazing Foreman and making his eyes swell. Moorer would throw a left. Foreman would answer with a hard right. This was no lightweight match. No sir. It was a classic for the ages, to go down as one of the greatest heavyweight bouts of all time.

Foreman's blows were draining Moorer of strength with each round. He knew it was simply a matter of time before his opponent would leave an opening for a knockout punch. If he could find that crack in Moorer's armor, it would give him the shot for a left hook. That would be his ticket home.

By the end of the ninth round Moorer was far ahead on points because of his relentless jabs. If the fight went the distance, he would win on the judges' scorecards. But Foreman was determined that wasn't going to happen. He threw a series of left hooks in the tenth round that weakened Moorer, making it harder for him to defend himself. Every time Foreman connected on a body shot, it took a little more strength out of Moorer. Moorer was wobbling, his legs getting weaker. The time was right. If Foreman could knock him down now, his opponent wouldn't be able to get up. Foreman connected "a hard right to Moorer's forehead with such force that it made [his] hand hurt." Still the stubborn Moorer didn't go down! "What kind of man can take that sort of blow to the head and still remain standing?" thought Foreman.[1] But he knew it wouldn't be long, so he didn't let up.

Then it happened. A crack opened in the armor.

Moorer ducked when Foreman threw a powerful left hook, which allowed Foreman to follow up with a quick right. BAM! It was the punch that sent Moorer to the canvas! As the referee started counting, Foreman stepped back. He knew the party was over. Michael Moorer wasn't getting back up. For the second time in his life, George Foreman was boxing's heavyweight champion of the world. This time, however, instead of gloating and boasting, he humbly went to his corner, dropped to his knees, and thanked God for the victory. It was quite the contrast to his first championship in

1973, when Foreman defeated Smokin' Joe Frazier in the Sunshine Showdown. It was twenty-one years later, and things had changed. George was a new man with a new mission.

You Can't Do That

When after a decade in retirement George Foreman made the decision to make a comeback at nearly forty years of age, his friends thought he'd lost his mind. "You can't do that," they said. Sure, he had been the heavyweight champion of the world way back in 1973, but that was a long time ago. Think about it—most professional boxers hang up their gloves somewhere between their late twenties and midthirties. The same is true in many professional sports. Occasionally some last until their late thirties. Rarely will an athlete last until forty. But that's when they stop, not start over! George Foreman was starting over.

The boxing experts were certain he was too old and out of shape. "Those young guys will kill you!" they warned. The great Gil Clancy, who had at one time been George's trainer, said, "Boxing has too many retreads. What is George Foreman doing out there boxing? He shouldn't be fighting."[2] Others said that instead of being in the ring, he should be on a respirator! No one gave him a chance. In essence they were saying, "Stay put, George. Stay down. Don't get back up." Foreman stood his ground, though. He let others laugh and doubt all they wanted, but Foreman knew he had God in his corner, fueling him. God was the One he listened to. With God's power George Foreman defied the critics and, at age forty-five, became the heavyweight champion of the world, "the oldest person ever to capture the title"![3]

In the ring one day back in the 1970s, after getting pounded for several rounds, Foreman staggered to the stool in his corner and plopped down. His manager, Gil Clancy, began slapping him in the face. "George!" he shouted. "Do you want it? George, do you really want it!"[4] At that moment, Foreman had to decide whether he would keep fighting—he had to choose between surrendering to the pain or getting back up and fighting to the end. It was up to him. Nobody was going to do it for him. Did he really want it? Did he really want to go the distance? Clancy's question became a key to how Foreman faced his battles: Do you really want it?

Years later, though, after having lost it all through a boatload of mistakes—youthful arrogance, poor decisions, financial investments going south, ruined relationships, anger issues, and selfish living—something happened. Foreman had an authentic encounter with the God of the universe. His motto changed from "You have to really want it" to "Take it back by God's power, not my own." After praying about it, Foreman felt God was leading him to come out of retirement and climb back into the ring, which meant it would have to be a God thing for him to succeed. If God didn't come through, he'd be dead meat. But unlike before, his motives were now pursuing a vision from God (which included funding the George Foreman Youth and Community Center), committing to his church and his family, and being a godly example for his children and the world. Instead of the world's superstars as his role models, his role models were now Jesus, the men of the Bible, and men in his life who were full of the Holy Spirit. And just like something rose up in King David to fight the giant Goliath thousands of years earlier in ancient Israel, something rose up in George Foreman. It was a stirring inside him to be the man, the father, and the boxer he was created to be. He wanted to do it right the second time around. After recapturing the heavyweight crown, the sports world was in disbelief—but not George. He knew who he was as a man, and he knew who the ultimate source of his strength was.

It's no secret that men today are getting a bad rap. They are being painted as buffoons, absentee dads, porn addicts, and toxic people. But the truth is the world desperately depends upon real men rising up in times of need. Right now, more than ever, God is calling men to be men. In a culture that wants to feminize them and keep them down, men need to know who they are, that God created them fully masculine, and who their ultimate source of strength is. It's time to rediscover the soul of a man.

DISCUSSION QUESTIONS

Are you worn down from the relentless jabs and punches that life and the culture are throwing at you? How so?

Do you feel irrelevant as a man, as if it's too late for you? Explain.

What things tempt you to just stay in your corner or stay down on the mat?

In what ways are you being stirred as a man to rise up?

SWORD OF THE WORD

Be strong, and show yourself a man.

—1 KINGS 2:2

PRAY ABOUT IT

Pray and ask God to help you remember that He is your ultimate source of strength.

CHAPTER 2

Men Matter

When a man lives up to his role, life-giving things
start to happen....Every family and societal problem
can get better when a man knows how to fulfill his
role and takes action....In life, we men cannot
afford to blow our assignments. It's not merely a
team that is counting on us; it's all of society.

—RODERICK L. HAIRSTON

IN THE LAST scene in the classic movie *Saving Private Ryan*, James Ryan is an aging man, standing in the Normandy American Cemetery and Memorial in front of the cross marking the grave of Captain John H. Miller, the man who had led the search team to locate him and bring him home during World War II. Private Ryan was one of four brothers, three of whom had been killed in action. When General George Marshall learned of this, he sent orders to Captain Miller and his men to find Private Ryan somewhere in France and bring him home. Miller and several of his men lost their lives in the effort. At the gravesite years later, Ryan flashes back to that moment on the bridge in Normandy when Captain Miller died. Ryan had actually relived that moment almost every day of his entire life. As Captain Miller was fading away from gunshot wounds, he pulled young Private Ryan close and whispered into his ear, words slow and labored, "James...Earn this...earn it." In that final scene, kneeling before Captain Miller's grave, Ryan says, "Every day I think about what you said to me that day on the bridge....I hope that at least in your eyes I've earned what all of you have done for me." When his wife walks up to his side, Ryan looks at her and says, "Tell me I've led a good life....Tell me I'm a good man."

She touches his cheek and says, "You are." After she walks away, Ryan stands at attention and salutes the grave. It's an all-time epic movie ending.

I saw this movie after my father-in-law, Clay, found out he had cancer. He and I were out shopping with my wife, Julie, and her mom. The girls were doing their thing, and we two guys were bored out of our minds. We were twiddling our thumbs, so I said, "Let's go watch that movie *Saving Private Ryan*. I hear it's pretty good."

"OK," Clay said.

Neither one of us had a clue what was about to happen. The movie was incredibly powerful, but that final scene punched us in the face. We came out of the theater different. A shift in us took place. It had that kind of impact. As a result of what happened on the bridge back in 1944, James Ryan lived a life of pressure. So should all men. I know that's probably not a popular thing to say. After all, we are to rest in God's grace and provision for us at the cross. We can't save ourselves and must come to the end of ourselves and reach out for Christ, our only hope. "For by grace you have been saved through faith. And this is not your own doing; it is the gift of God, not a result of works, so that no one may boast."[1]

While this is true, as men we are made to battle in a state of divine tension. Temptations, our own flesh, the challenges of life, and the culture are all fighting against us, trying to get us to break down and then stay down. Yet God can use those pressures to goad us into rising up to the occasions around us. "Faith thrives in holy discomfort," said Louie Giglio.[2] In essence what Ryan was asking himself and his wife was, "Did I make my life count? Did I matter? Did I make a difference? Did I rise to the occasion?" These are the same questions men are asking themselves today.

Some years back my son, Zach and I found ourselves walking through Arlington National Cemetery when we were visiting Washington, DC. Zach was about thirteen, and it was just the two of us. Very few people were there. When we got out of our car, I told Zach what the cemetery was all about. "Dad," he said, "I've never seen so many white crosses." We began to walk, and it got really quiet between the two of us. Few words were spoken as an aura of sacredness hung thick in the air. As we wove our way through the cemetery toward the Tomb of the Unknown Soldier, a military funeral was going on with soldiers in dress blues firing a gun salute. We had to stop and stand. Zach stood beside me as we watched this family bury their kid and pay tribute to him.

There was silence.

There was reverence.

There was honor.

Finally we made our way up to the Tomb of the Unknown Soldier. As we stood there, Zach saw the guards and the aura and the history of all those who served and gave the ultimate sacrifice. Because freedom is not free. It costs something. Someone had to pay the price. That's what we do in this life. We give tribute and honor and value to those who served. We don't minimize those works. We call ourselves to that same level of servitude in life. We call ourselves to that same standard. As my boy and I stood there, we could hear taps playing in the distance. Tears welled up. Another family just buried their son or daughter.

Up in the hills of rural Pennsylvania, there's this place close to my old homestead where we go hunting. While driving up there with Zach, we passed by the home of one of my best friends growing up. I told Zach, "That's where Joe lived, son. Look right there on that hill." On the hill near the country home is a flagpole with the American flag blowing in the wind. Lights are shining up on it. "That's called Brad's Hill. It's a memorial to a fallen soldier. Brad, who was one of America's finest, was killed in Iraq. He was Joe's sister's son. He is buried in Arlington Cemetery. Every day, his family looks at the reminder of the sacrifice of their son so we can live and do this. I'm sure they cry for him every day. No, son, freedom is not free. It costs something."

Do men matter?

Those men did. To keep America safe and free, it takes sacrifice. It takes men.

According to history, men are the scale tippers, the spurs that get the horses moving, the rudders that turn ships, and the protectors. Without the influence of strong, masculine men, society goes astray. John Hawkins wrote in his article "5 Reasons Masculinity Is Increasingly Coming Under Attack in America":

> The very traits that the APA [American Psychological Association] says are so harmful…are the same traits that built the entire world. If anything, saying that 98 percent of the great industrialists, scientists, generals, inventors, heroes, and leaders have been men with traditional masculine values is an UNDERSTATEMENT. Who created the Constitution? Who won every war America has ever fought? Who put men on the moon? Who built the internet you're reading this article on? Men with traditional masculine values. When you say that is unhealthy or that we don't need them anymore, you are thoughtlessly discarding the engine that built almost the entirety of civilization.[3]

When I was growing up near Clearfield, Pennsylvania, my older brother Jimmy signed up for the military—the US Marines. As a boy in the car with my dad, a World War II veteran, we would drive into town and pass this big sign on the corner by the courthouse that said, "The US Marines: We're looking for a few good men." Every time I saw it, something would *rise up* inside me. Even at that young age, I wanted to be counted as one of those few good men, just like my dad and my brother. Wanting to be good men was in our blood.

As a professional counselor and coach, I often hear the men I work with ask questions like these (you probably guessed them): "Am I one of the few?" "Am I a good man?" "Do I matter?"

DISCUSSION QUESTIONS

As a man, do you personally feel you matter, or do you feel that you really don't matter? Explain.

What are some specific roles, both big and small, you play that make a difference in those around you?

What does being a good man mean to you? Do you see yourself as a good man?

The Bible says that none of us is good.[4] We all have a sin nature and fall short of God's perfect standard. How do we reconcile being a good man with God's Word?

What is a good man in God's eyes?

SWORD OF THE WORD

> For by grace you have been saved through faith. And this is not your own doing; it is the gift of God.
> —EPHESIANS 2:8

PRAY ABOUT IT

If you are struggling to believe that your life matters, ask God to show you some areas where you have made a difference.

CHAPTER 3

God Is Looking for a Man

It is not an accident that [David] went from the sheep fold to the throne. Success like that never comes about by mere chance. . . . Manhood—true manhood—princely manhood, like that of David, is one of the grandest things in the world, and it is something that counts as nothing else does. . . . To be a man means to be strong in purpose and self-control. If your manhood is buried under doubt, dig it out.

—BILLY SUNDAY

JUST LIKE THE Marines are looking for a few good men, so is God. He is looking for men after His heart who will do what He wants them to do. "I have found David son of Jesse," the Bible tells us, "a man after my own heart; he will do everything I want him to do."[1] The "I" in that passage is God. What's interesting about this scripture is that it starts with "I have *found* David." That means God was looking. He was looking not just for any man but for a man after His own heart, who would do His will. I don't know about you, but at the end of my life that's how I want to be remembered. Really, nothing else matters. More than being a good man, I want to be a "God" man. That's what real manhood is all about. It's quite possible to be a good man and not be a "God" man.

Authentic manhood is about the heart—God's heart.

A man can know God's heart. Let that sink in.

David was a warrior-king who knew incredible victories as well as heartbreaking defeats. He knew God in the wilderness when shepherding sheep with vicious predators stalking them and when he slew the giant warrior-champion Goliath. He knew God when hiding out in the caves of Adullam and when reigning in the palace. He experienced euphoric spiritual highs, yet he fell to the lowest, deepest pits of sin, despair, and self-loathing. He had loyal kids who adored him and kids who wanted him dead. David's life ran the full gamut of ups and downs, joys and sorrows. As a warrior-king he was responsible for much bloodshed.[2] David also fell into adultery with Bathsheba. Then, after discovering she was pregnant, he arranged for her husband, Uriah, to be put into a vulnerable battle position, which led to Uriah's death.[3] Against God's law, David had multiple wives.[4] Because of his reckless fathering, his family suffered inner conflict and misfortune.[5] In addition, David disobediently numbered his military after God specifically told him not to. The result was seventy thousand of his people perishing in a plague.[6]

All of the above is true, yet three consistent themes ran throughout David's life. Three things never changed.

David was fully man with feet of clay that were marred and cracked.

David loved God.

David knew God.

The obvious questions I'm sure many of you are asking are "How could this be? How can a man love God and sin like that, and how can God bless a man with that kind of sin?" I am certainly not excusing David's actions. Neither is God. As we will see in a later chapter, David also knew true sorrow and repentance for his sin and failures. Author Jim George wrote in his book *A Man After God's Own Heart*:

How could God possibly commend a man with this kind of background? Yes, David was a man with feet of clay, a man who at times committed sins that most of us could not imagine, let alone commit. Yet over the long haul, David sought to be righteous and his heart's desire was to do God's will. This is the kind of man God was looking for as indicated by Jeremiah 5:1 [NIV]: "Go up and down the streets of Jerusalem, look around and consider, search through her squares. If you can find but one person who deals honestly and seeks the truth, I will forgive this city." God doesn't expect perfection, as we can clearly see from David. With all that David had done wrong in his life, God could still look at David's heart and say he was a man after His own heart—a man who did all God's will.[7]

"If you, O LORD, should mark iniquities, O Lord, who could stand?" penned David. "But with you there is forgiveness, that you may be feared."[8] I love that, and I want that. David knew that righteousness, like Abraham's, could come only through faith in God's mercy. He understood and looked forward to the coming Messiah. David also wrote, "The LORD taketh pleasure in them that fear him, in those that hope in his mercy."[9] David knew God when he was disciplined by Him, and then he found cleansing and forgiveness. It's possible to know God, love Him deeply, and still fail Him miserably. That was David. That is us.

Yet he was a man *after* God's own heart. God found him, but David chased *after* God to do His will. "As the deer pants for the water brooks," wrote David, "so my soul pants for You, O God. My soul thirsts for God, for the living God."[10] Even though David is not named as the author of Psalm 42, scholars conclude it is from his hand. It is Davidic in nature and maintains the elements of his style. The point is that God is looking for men who thirst and pant for Him, men who will step forward in those God moments, men who will rise up and do His will.

Prove Yourself a Man

Around 970 BC, as David's time on earth drew to a close, there was
so much he could say, so many truths to convey before passing the
baton of leadership to Solomon, his son. Solomon was waiting by his
father's side, listening, grieving, and knowing time with him was lim-
ited. Father to son, David began with "I go the way of all the earth; be
strong, therefore, and prove yourself a man."[11] The giant slayer, the
warrior-king, and the man after God's own heart, David knew that
effective leadership began with the foundation of being a *man*. Yet
the type of manhood he was talking about didn't simply happen as a
result of testosterone and perhaps the ability to wield a sword. King
Saul, who reigned before David, possessed all of that, but he was not
a man after God's heart. He had the physical stature and was charismatic, handsome, and a great warrior, but he let his ego, pride, and
self-sufficiency lead to his fall. Saul had many toxic characteristics
and behaviors that were not repented of and submitted to God.

David, on the other hand, was talking to his son Solomon about
manhood that was to be demonstrated and proven by godly character. In short, proving himself a man meant Solomon was to
embrace God's definition of *manhood* and to be strong in the face of
adversity. David knew what was coming. He understood that Israel's
many enemies, from without and within, would be launching full-
frontal attacks against them. Solomon would need to man up
by making godly choices. To lead efficiently, he needed to see his
source was God, not his own strength. Solomon's brother Absalom
sadly went the same route as Saul. He trusted in his ego and brute
strength instead of in God. Absalom was a high-strung, rebellious
man who thought too highly of himself. Narcissistic at his core, he
was ruled by his elevated sense of self and thoughts of grandeur and
power. He even had a monument erected to honor himself. In the
end Absalom wound up swinging by his hair from a tree limb, wide

open to his opponent's attack.[12] How many men today are lost in and trapped by their own egos and behaviors, leaving themselves wide open and vulnerable to the enemy's attacks?

David understood that as Israel's new leader, Solomon would need to take a stand, leading the people in keeping God's ways. His leadership of Israel, however, had to begin with his own personal integrity before God. David's deathbed exhortation to his son continued: "And keep the charge of the LORD your God: to walk in His ways, to keep His statutes, His commandments, His judgments, and His testimonies, as it is written in the Law of Moses, that you may prosper in all that you do and wherever you turn."[13] According to David, Solomon proving himself a man and being an effective leader started with embracing God's plan and walking in His ways.

David related authentic manhood to serving God. That's big.

The same is true today. For men to impact the culture around them and their circles of influence, starting with their families, they must embrace God's true definition of *manhood* and *masculinity*. You don't have to accept mainstream media's or some liberal organization's label of who you are, and you certainly don't have to accept the mischaracterized version of traditional masculinity—but instead you must accept the absolute truth of what God's Word says about you. J. Oswald Sanders wrote, "When God does discover a man who conforms to His spiritual requirement, who is willing to pay the full price of discipleship, He uses him to the limit, despite his patent shortcomings."[14] The great need of our culture today is not for more men of talent or more men of success but for more men of character with hearts that follow hard after God. Our culture needs men who have taken up David's challenge to Solomon to "be strong, therefore, and prove yourself a man" and who understand what that means.

Yes, God is looking for a man.

Will He find you?

DISCUSSION QUESTIONS

What is the condition of your heart? Are you chasing after God, panting for Him? How so?

What do you see as your source—God or your own strength and willpower? Explain.

Will you step out and follow God in the face of adversity? Why or why not?

SWORD OF THE WORD

My soul thirsts for God, for the living God.

—Psalm 42:2

PRAY ABOUT IT

The Word says, "Blessed are those who hunger and thirst for righteousness, for they shall be satisfied."[15] Ask the Lord to give you a hunger and thirst for Him and then to fill you until you are completely satisfied in Him.

CHAPTER 4

Walls and Gatekeepers

*To see a man beaten not by a better
opponent but by himself is a tragedy.*

—CUS D'AMATO

MAGINE THE SCENE. Their city had been decimated. Thin lines of
smoke twisted upward to the heavens from the blackened ruins
of what was left of their homes. The smell of ash hung thick in the
air, making it difficult to breathe. Some coughed. Some gagged. All
wept. Their enemies had done their work, each smoldering pile an
offering to their pagan gods.

Just hours earlier jubilation had filled the hearts of king-to-be
David and his band of men as they drew closer to home after a
three-day trek into the wilderness, doing what warriors do. But the
joy would soon be overtaken by panic as the men topped the rocky
mountain ledge overlooking the valley where their hometown of
Ziklag lay in the distance. The slithering lines of smoke ascending
in the far background were a sure sign that something dreadful had
occurred. Spurred in the sides, the horses jolted from a casual gait
to a full-fledged gallop, dust and rocks kicking up behind them.

Upon arriving in Ziklag, the men were horrified to find that the
city had been raided and torched, their valuables stolen—supplies,
weapons, gold, herds. It was the Amalekites, barbaric plunderers

known for cruel, ruthless, unrelenting brutality, doing all sorts of detestable things the Lord God hates, even burning their own sons and daughters as sacrifices to their false gods.

Weaving through the damage, the men realized something else was amiss. The atmosphere was eerily quiet, save the sound of their own horses' hoofbeats, dogs barking somewhere in the void, and angry embers crackling. No one was there, crying out to greet them. No women or children were running grief-stricken in the streets. No one was bent down by the piles of rubble, wailing. Then it hit them. The town was vacant, and their most valued treasure had been stolen—their wives and their sons and daughters had been taken captive. When men let their walls down, the enemy is right there waiting to make its move—and the consequences are dire.

As the full weight of what happened fell upon them, the men began to weep. Some dropped their weapons, slipped from their saddles, and fell to their knees, wailing. Others beat their chests and yelled, the deep agonizing cries of fury echoing throughout the valley.

They wept for their wives, for their sons, for their daughters.[1]

They wept for themselves and for all they had lost.

The Bible says they "wept aloud until they had no strength left to weep."[2]

One of the misconceptions about masculinity is that real men don't cry. Not true. Not biblical. These guys who wept were about as tough as you could get. Let's just say that there was no shortage of testosterone in the group. They were courageous and battle tested. Robust and wild at heart, they were men's men who had banded together with David to rise up against the oppression and wickedness of King Saul. They wanted their culture back, and they wanted Israel to serve God again. They were men of valor who eventually became known as David's "mighty men."[3]

Among them were guys such as Josheb-basshebeth, who took out eight hundred of the enemy in one battle with a spear. Eleazar stayed on the battlefield when other warriors fled. He fought Philistines until his hand was stuck, clenched around his sword. There was Abishai, who killed three hundred men with a spear, and Benaiah, who jumped down into a pit on a snowy day and killed a lion. He also wrestled a powerful Egyptian man, killing him with the man's own spear.[4] Some of the other men who joined David were ambidextrous, having the ability to use both the right hand and the left in hurling stones, using spears, and shooting arrows.[5] This was a big deal when in combat. They could do double the damage. These men knew how to fight a battle and win.

With all their power and skill and character, they still wept.

Sometimes real men need to weep. We need to weep for our past, for our families, for what has happened to our nation, for what we've allowed to happen. We need to cry out to God for our wives and children, our brothers and sisters. We need to be broken and mourn over our own sin. If we take care of personal stuff, it influences the church and the nation. Jared Mulvihill wrote:

> Yes, we should be weeping. We should be appalled, disgusted, shocked, and grieved in the depths of our hearts over our sin. All our sin is treason against God. Not just the prideful, lying, stealing, and lusting sins but sins of the tongue, sins of anxiousness, sins of bitterness, sins of partiality, sins of complacency, sins of jealousy, sins of impatience, and sins of arrogance. We should grieve over them all.[6]

It's time to be honest about our lives and the desolation around us. It's time to grieve, to be angered in our spirits, and most importantly to rise up!

Like David and his band of men, weeping and grief over what we have lost and repentance should be our first response too. Whether we shed actual tears isn't the point. There must be authentic repentance in our hearts that leads to lasting change. Change begins in the heart. It's a gut-level, core initiative. Second Corinthians 7:10 says, "Godly sorrow brings repentance that leads to salvation and leaves no regret, but worldly sorrow brings death" (NIV). Some 180 years ago, Charles Finney put it this way: "What is the testimony of your closet? Can it bear witness to your sighs and groans and tears over the wickedness and desolations of the world?"[7]

"Draw near to God, and he will draw near to you," declares James. "Cleanse your hands, you sinners, and purify your hearts, you double-minded. Be wretched and mourn and weep. Let your laughter be turned to mourning and your joy to gloom."[8] There's no nice, easy, soft way to put it. James isn't sugarcoating anything here. He wants us to grasp the full gravity and wretchedness of our sin and the sin that is all around us. James wrote like a man who doesn't have time to beat around the bush—and neither do we. Men must take responsibility and feel the weight of their actions. David and his men did. This was their first step to taking back what the enemy had stolen.

How Could the Tragedy of Ziklag Even Happen?

The tragedy of Ziklag happened because the men were out of the picture. It was their own fault. There's no other way to say it. The men let the tragedy of Ziklag happen. They could have prevented it. For a brief period of three days they let down the walls of protection, which left everything vulnerable to attack, and the enemy seized the opportunity. One has to ask, How could they even allow such a thing? I mean, they were seasoned warriors who knew perfectly well that their enemies were lurking about, just waiting for an opportunity.

The truth is that David and his band of men got overconfident and let their personal guards down. David, who normally leaned on and pressed into God, relaxed a bit and did life his own way. This included making a couple deals with another enemy, the Philistines, out of his fleshly wisdom. It would cost him dearly. Though he never left his love for God or even doubted he was God's anointed, David at times strayed from his total dependence on God as his source of strength and direction. In fact David had been doing things his own way for a year and four months, living out of the will of God for that time.[9] He must have figured he could walk in his fleshly wisdom and go about his life depending on his own power and insight with no consequences.

Wrong.

There are always consequences when we try to do life independently, without seeking God's counsel. One of the weaknesses of many men—maybe most men—is at times they want to go it alone, to do it on their own, to be independent. That independence can be a double-edged sword. Been there and done that a few times!

As men we must live a life of seeking God, walking in the Spirit, and renewing our dependence on Him. If we don't, we will miss it—we will blow it. David and his band of men did. Not depending on God's direction for those sixteen months led to a big blunder and the three-day lapse in judgment of leaving Ziklag unprotected. The enemy was right there waiting to rush in and take their most treasured assets. Hear me: our adversary is very patient. Big acts of sin and lapses in judgment that bring us down rarely "just happen." They are a result of our personal walls being broken down over time and our drifting away from dependence on God. Because these mighty men's personal walls of protection were down, they failed in their ability to protect. You see, the men *were* the walls of protection.

When Men Let Their Guards Down

I believe the same is true today. Men are to be the walls of protection around those God has placed in their lives. What's interesting about Ziklag is when the men let their guards down by leaving the city unprotected, their wives, sons, and daughters could not defend themselves against the evil onslaught. Otherwise they would never have been taken captive. Ponder that for a moment. When men let their guards down, the wives, sons, and daughters are left unprotected. That's because men are called to be the gatekeepers. It's the way God set it up. Ezekiel 22:30 says, "So I sought for *a man* among them who would *make a wall*, and *stand in the gap* before Me on behalf of the land" (NKJV, emphasis added). God is looking for men who will be a wall, who will stand in the gap and be gatekeepers. Yet for men to *be* the walls of protection, they must *have* strong personal walls. "A man without self-control is like a city broken into and left without walls."[10] When a man has no self-control of his own spirit and body, the enemy rushes in and plunders his city, tearing down the walls of protection. After corrupting the soul of a man and breaking down his personal walls of protection, the enemy proceeds to steal his valuables—time, purpose, dignity, integrity, and security—and then wreaks havoc within his most important relationships. When our personal walls are broken down, the enemy comes in to destroy us. And then after we are weakened and out of the picture, he can take out our treasures. Do you see the connection between personal walls and being a wall? You have to have the first to be the second. It is the man's responsibility to stand in the gap and be the walls of protection for his family and the important people in his life.

When a man's life falls into disorder, when his personal walls are broken down, it impacts more than just him. It impacts his city—his individual circle of influence. Walls aren't always made of brick or stone. Sometimes they are made of flesh. They are a spiritual barricade. For the enemy to get to the valuables in your city, he must come through you. When you are the wall, you can't afford to wander off in the wilderness for three days. When the enemy entices you to indulge in online porn, to cheat on that business deal, to pursue those selfish pleasures that always end in destruction, consider the fallout and how it will impact you and all the people you love. Maybe that's why Jesus said to "count the cost."[11]

The enemy will wait and wait and wait and lull us into complacency and then—BAM!—ambush us like a predator striking its prey.[12] Isn't that where men get into trouble? We convince ourselves we have everything under control and slack off from keeping ourselves anchored and seeking God. We do life our own way, thinking we can handle it in our own strength and wisdom or that we're too busy to spend time with the Lord. "The biggest battle you will face in life," said Ravi Zacharias, "is keeping your daily appointment with God; keep it, or every other battle becomes bigger."[13]

When a boxer leaves himself unguarded, his opponent will seize the opportunity to deliver the knockout punch, just as George Foreman did with Michael Moorer. Our opponent is also patiently waiting for us to allow an opening he can take advantage of. As with David and his band of men, often it's a subtle shift, almost a subconscious drifting. We get lazy or tired and then distracted. We let our own flesh, coupled with the enemy, lure us into thinking we have everything covered, when in reality our focus is divided, our walls are broken down, and our gates are left wide open. When we insist on doing life on our own, we get lost—we lose, and the ones we love the most lose too. Spending time seeking God must be a priority. It's the most important thing. When we keep God first, He helps order our lives so those things that He values most are what we value most and spend our time on.

Look at the world around you. Walls are broken down mostly because men's personal walls are broken down and they have left the scene. This has allowed the enemy to waltz in and take captive their most prized possessions. We've seen the devastating effects of what happens when men are out of the picture. We know the enemy wants to strip us of our masculinity and take us out. Why? It's because men matter. They are the walls.

Walls protect what we care about the most.

This is why now more than ever men need strong personal walls.

DISCUSSION QUESTIONS

What are you grieved about or weeping over?

Are you taking responsibility for your actions? How so?

What is the condition of your personal wall?

Are you walking in dependence on God? Do you look to Him in all the areas of your life—your wife, family, and career? Why or why not?

What has the enemy stolen from you? What are some things you might need to do to rebuild your personal wall?

SWORD OF THE WORD

> I sought for a man among them who should build up the wall and stand in the breach before me for the land.
> —Ezekiel 22:30

PRAY ABOUT IT

Ask God to show you the places where your personal wall is in disrepair, leaving you vulnerable to attack. Then ask Him how to fix the wall.

CHAPTER 5

Take It Back!

Courage is being scared to death and saddling up anyway.
—ATTRIBUTED TO JOHN WAYNE

Now, here's the really cool part about the scene at Ziklag. In the midst of the chaos, the brokenness, the ruin, David went to God on his knees. Once David repented, made things right with God, and strengthened himself in the Lord, he knew he had God's ear. There was a clear line of communication. He was not going to make the same mistake again and move on his own without God's direction. David cried out to God again. Only this time he asked God, "What do I do?"

> So David inquired of the LORD, saying, "Shall I pursue this troop? Shall I overtake them?"[1]

The Lord God heard David's cries, as He will yours, and answered him: "Pursue, for you shall surely overtake them and without fail recover all."[2] In other words, "Rally your men, son! Saddle up your horses! Go get it! Take it back—and don't just get some of it. Get all of it!" God's not into doing anything halfway.

At our last men's conference I sensed a shift. You could feel it. God was at work, and I believe He was telling His men the same thing. "Saddle up! It's time. Be warriors for Me, and take it back!

Take back everything the enemy has stolen! Take back what you allowed to be stolen. Don't settle." God was fully aware of the mistakes David and his men had made, yet He was still with them. He will be with you too. The enemy is lying when he says, "It's too late. You've messed up too much." That is not true. In fact God can supernaturally redeem what has been lost to make you stronger. Your past truly isn't your past if it's still affecting your present. Stop beating yourself up about the past. Ask God what to do and where to go from here to redeem your mistakes.

There are two parallel themes weaving throughout this book:

1. How men can take back what they have lost on a personal level—rebuilding their individual walls of protection; developing integrity, holiness, accountability, and godliness; and embracing their masculinity, the way God created them, without apology

2. How to take back what we've lost in our relationships and as a nation and the key role men have in reclaiming the culture—showing up in our circles of influence, giving to something bigger than ourselves, and letting that circle expand one person at a time

Taking back your life personally and taking back the culture are tightly linked. The second can't happen until the first happens. But with God's authority and favor it will happen. When David rallied his men, I believe they could see the resolve and confidence he had after connecting with God. Once again they chose to follow one whose face reflected authority and power. In that moment the men began to release their bitterness and anger toward David and channel it, refocusing it toward the goal. They could see and sense God's favor on their leader. The same will happen to you. When you strengthen yourself in the Lord, the people around you will begin to notice and have confidence in your steps to new life. When David said, "We must go and fight and take it all back!" they took action.

They did something.

We must do something.

There is a time to weep.

There is a time to seek God's face.

Then there is a time to dry the tears, grab your sword, and do battle!

That's what David and his mighty warriors did. They went on a rampage! It would be great if we could say all six hundred men fought valiantly and overcame. But the ride wasn't easy. David pushed so hard that two hundred men never made it to the battle-field. Weak and weary, they dropped out of the fight. But it didn't dissuade David. He and the remaining men chased down the Amalekites, cleaned them out, and took back what the enemy had stolen plus more![3] I like the way *The Message* describes it:

> David pounced. He [and his men] fought them from before sunrise until evening of the next day. None got away except for four hundred of the younger men who escaped by riding off on camels. David rescued everything the Amalekites had taken. And he rescued his two wives! Nothing and no one was missing—young or old, son or daughter, plunder or whatever. David recovered the whole lot. He herded the sheep and cattle before them, and they all shouted, "David's plunder!"[4]

Sometimes you have to get fed up and then get fired up!

You have to pounce.

It is time. Enough is enough. Change has to happen, and it has to happen now.

Will you drop out because you are weary and discouraged, or will you strengthen yourself in the Lord and press on in the fight?

On September 11, 2001, United Airlines flight 93 was somewhere over Pennsylvania when hijacked by terrorists. The passengers found out that other planes had crashed into the World Trade Center and the Pentagon. They realized that the terrorists' plan was to use their plane as a missile targeting perhaps the White House or Capitol in Washington, DC. Thirty-two-year-old Todd Beamer, along with Mark Bingham, Tom Burnett, and Jeremy Glick, knew it was time to rise up and take action to stop another major terrorist attack from happening. After the men contemplated, they knew what had to be done, even though it would mean the loss of their own lives. Courageously the men formed a plan and surged forward to retake the plane from the hijackers. As the attack began, Todd Beamer stated those famous words, "Let's roll," and the men took action. They stepped into the moment. Flight 93 crashed that day in the hills of central Pennsylvania and no one survived, but as a result hundreds, if not thousands, of lives were saved.

God is calling out to men today.

It is time to fight.

Saddle up your horses, men.

Let's roll!

DISCUSSION QUESTIONS

When you blow it, do you run from God or to God?

How do you think David strengthened himself in the Lord?

How do you personally hear from God for direction?

Is there any anger and bitterness in your heart that's keeping you from saddling up? Explain.

What would you have done if you were on Flight 93? Are you willing to die for something bigger than yourself?

SWORD OF THE WORD

Pursue, for you shall surely overtake them and without fail recover all.

—1 Samuel 30:8, nkjv

PRAY ABOUT IT

Inquire of the Lord just as David did. Ask Him what to do and how to do it.

CHAPTER 6
A Vicious Opponent

*The heart is the truth of your identity, that's why
the gods fight so fiercely for every inch of it.*
—KYLE IDLEMAN

IN CASE YOU haven't noticed, there's a vicious opponent of masculinity dancing around the cultural ring these days, taking relentless jabs and throwing serious punches at men and their God-given identities. Our country is locked in a slugfest where good and evil are pitted against each other and men are smack-dab in the middle. Instead of celebrating manhood, our opponent is set on idolizing and glorifying what isn't manly at all while demonizing authentic masculinity. Understand, this adversary *hates* masculinity and wants to redefine how God created us. If you embrace conservative principles, including traditional masculinity, those throwing these punches don't merely disagree with you—they want to humiliate, embarrass, and shame you and knock you out of the fight. Traditional masculinity is their enemy and viewed as toxic. Below are just a few of the actual headlines I came across while writing this book:

- "Conservative Speaker Says 'Men Are Not Women,' Is Attacked, Sprayed With Chemical"[1]

- "Traditional Masculinity Can Hurt Boys, Say New A.P.A. Guidelines"[2]

- "This Father's Day, Men Are Experiencing a Crisis of Masculinity. The Solution? More Feminism."[3]

- "Toxic Masculinity in Boys Is Fueling an Epidemic of Loneliness"[4]

- "It's Time for Drag Kings to Detoxify Masculinity on TV"[5]

- "Terry Crews: 'Masculinity Can Be a Cult'"[6]

- "Raise Boys as Feminists to Change 'Culture of Sexism,' Says Justin Trudeau"[7]

Hundreds of headlines like these are pounding the world daily, and it has taken a toll on our men, boys, and even women. Really, things have gotten so rough for traditional men that they are not merely on the ropes and on the verge of being knocked out; they're on the verge of dying—their voices and influence eliminated, snuffed out, dead. This is precisely what the opposition wants and is targeting.

On October 16, 2019, during the writing of this book, Golden Gloves champion Patrick Day died as a result of a traumatic brain injury. He went into a coma after receiving relentless blows to the head in a boxing match four days earlier.[8] Likewise, men today can't take much more berating, defamation, reproach, and insults, or we will end up with similar tragic results. We've got to start delivering our own counterpunches! "I'm not saying that men should go around spoiling for a fight," wrote Gordon Dalbey, "but that we be prepared to respond when God reveals to us the fight that He has equipped us to win."[9] And God has equipped men to win. There's no reason for us to allow ourselves to be bullied.

The world needs us to step up, women need it, and our sons and daughters need it.

A group of us guys were heading up to the Alaskan bush to do a little fishing and bonding in the wild. As we walked through the Anchorage airport, we saw a billboard of traditional masculine men dressed up in ballerina outfits. To me, it was a deliberate effort to humiliate and make regular joes look like buffoons. Personally offended, I thought, "What in the world?" There we were in camo and boots, going on a fishing trip, and there's this poster plastered on the wall that's the polar opposite of everything Alaska represents to me when it comes to men. It caught us completely off guard; it was like watching a clean family show that all of a sudden goes to a commercial of two guys kissing in a bed. You're looking at your wife and kids asking, "What just happened here?" You feel betrayed and totally set up. You know what I'm talking about. It turns your stomach. This is what our opponent is doing, trying to cram its ungodly agenda down our throats one way or another.

It's No Secret

It is no secret who our opponents are. They are those with the radical, liberal, progressive ideology and the enemy of all enemies that is behind it. Traditional masculinity is a threat to their system, so their goal is to silence and neuter the men who stand for traditional masculinity. At first it was only a small percentage of society, but now their poisonous message has infiltrated mainstream life, affecting nearly everyone. According to the American Psychological Association (APA), a secular organization, "Traditional masculinity is psychologically harmful."[10] What?! An op-ed on the subject asserted, "Forcing men to behave in accordance with the worst stereotypes of manliness harms them—and it harms others."[11] In other words, according to the APA, being manly is dangerous. I guess if you drive a pickup, fly a flag, ride a motorcycle, hunt, fish, like to compete, shoot a gun, and/or carry a Bible, you're the bad guy. Can you believe that? This is not some back-alley fringe organization promoting this. It's the top psychological organization in America. And this is how the indoctrination starts. It's happening in elementary school all the way through college. "When enough individuals are out of touch with the masculine, a whole society is weakened.... A crisis in masculinity is always a crisis in truth," said Leanne Payne.[12] This distorted view of masculinity is weakening our whole society. By the way, whenever the word *stereotypes* is used when describing men, it is almost always in a disparaging manner about common-sense, healthy, traditional biological definitions and most definitely about biblical standards. Of course, nothing could be further from the truth!

There has been an unprecedented misrepresentation of what true biblical manhood really looks like. There is also a concerted effort to vilify Christianity and for our country to rid itself of our Judeo-Christian heritage, including the God-given roles of men. Check out this blatant statement from a HuffPost article: "The faster conservative religion is overwhelmingly seen as mean, crazy, violent, hateful, misogynistic and anti-science, the faster we as a society can move on."[13] Notice that it is their goal to "move on" from conservative religious values—in other words, the God of the Bible. And to accomplish their goal, it's imperative that they make others view conservative values, including traditional masculinity, through their lens, however distorted, regardless of facts or of reality—and regardless of truth. When a lie is repeated long enough and often enough, people eventually start believing it, no matter how ridiculous it is. Notice that "misogynistic" is how they want conservative masculinity to be seen. Again, nothing could be further from the truth. It's a total mischaracterization.

An article in the Patriot Post, "Leftmedia's Deliberate

Mischaracterization of Christianity," concluded that "the vast majority of MSM [mainstream media] reporters have committed themselves to the promotion of the 'progressive' cause. And in so doing, they have created simplistic and flawed caricatures of those they revile, like Christians."[14] Sadly, that would include a flawed caricature of masculinity, including men in ballerina outfits looking pathetic. These caricatures have caused men to be the butt of jokes, shamed, made to look like buffoons, or painted as evil, insensitive, and sexist. All you have to do is turn on the television and watch the latest sitcoms and their commercials to confirm this. Instead of strong men such as those in *Braveheart* and *The Patriot*, traditional males today—fathers particularly—are more often than not portrayed as nitwits or chauvinistic. Their counterparts, however, are usually cool, quick-witted males who are heavily effeminate, not to mention often atheist with a sarcastic or condescending tone against those bigoted, mindless Christians and conservatives. Vicious progressives will stop at nothing to achieve their godless agenda. The good news is God's men have never backed down from a fight. In fact, throughout biblical and secular history, they've been called upon again and again to rise up and take it back. In this book we are going to look at some of them—guys such as David and his band of men, Nehemiah, Joseph, Josiah, Daniel, Samson, and Solomon, just to name a few, and of course Jesus. Until then we need to lay a foundation concerning this attack on men and masculinity.

DISCUSSION QUESTIONS

What is your understanding of godly, biblical manhood?

What can you do to combat the lies of society, media, and biased stereotypes within your family or environment?

Are you aware of those deliberate mischaracterizations of Christianity and the damage they cause? What are some examples?

If you are not moved or pricked by the assault on traditional, Christian values, is it because you've isolated yourself from the conflict? Why or why not? If you have isolated yourself from the conflict, do you want to pray for God to remove the blindness from your eyes and show you what you can do?

SWORD OF THE WORD

> The thief comes only to steal and kill and destroy. I came that they may have life and have it abundantly.
>
> —JOHN 10:10

PRAY ABOUT IT

Pray that God will show you the truth about who you are as a man, knowing that the truth will set you free.

CHAPTER 7

Another Crafty Enemy

*Any of us can easily slide into blaming our
circumstances [or others] for our sin....
Blame-shifting is as old as time. Starting with Adam,
men have been doing it almost since the very beginning.*

—JOHNNY HUNT

AFTER THE WEEPING at Ziklag, the men allowed another enemy to invade their camp. This one, however, was even craftier and more cunning than the Amalekites. It didn't wait for them to get out of the picture but slipped right in among them. It was the enemy of bitterness and blame. Instead of manning up and taking responsibility for their part in allowing the invasion to happen, the mighty warriors became so angry and resentful that they picked up stones and aimed them at their beloved leader. The Bible says, "David was greatly distressed because the men were talking of stoning him; each one was bitter in spirit because of his sons and daughters."[1] The grief that caused them to weep had now turned to bitterness. Instead of looking inward to examine their own hearts, they turned outward and seethed.

Yes, men must weep and mourn over what is happening in our hearts, lives, and homes and across our land, but we must be careful not to become bitter in spirit. "Fighting angry—that drains you twice as fast," said Tick Wills in the movie *Southpaw*.[2] Basically, if you fight with anger in your heart, you are going to get your butt handed to you. Anger has an insidious way of working into our hearts and minds to lock us up and paralyze us so we cannot take positive action. We become prisoners of the things and people that made us angry. That is a dangerous place to be. "Let all bitterness and wrath and anger and clamor and slander be put away from you, along with all malice," wrote the apostle Paul.[3] The writer of Hebrews wrote to beware, lest any "root of bitterness springs up, causing trouble."[4] Bitterness never brings about healing and restoration. Instead it makes us pick up stones. We can't hate the people within the systems that demonize men. We can't despise other men when they make mistakes or even sin. We can't despise ourselves. When we see the violence in society, when our loved ones get hurt, when our masculinity is threatened and painted as chauvinistic, when men exhibit toxic behavior—anger is a justified response to all these things. Yet, when that anger is turned into bitterness, it creates additional toxic behavior—such as men throwing stones at each other.

As men we mourn and weep about what is happening in our own lives first, then we take action. Anger is a God-given emotion to respond to real and personal issues in our lives. When we feel that we have been violated, whether it is real or perceived, or we see something that is not right, I believe God wired us as men to respond. Anger is best understood as a state of preparation to respond. Have you ever noticed that sometimes when we get angry, veins pop out in our foreheads and our nostrils get bigger? We clench our fists. Testosterone increases in our bodies. Our attention is focused. When we are mad, we can't think of anything else except what we are mad at. What we do with our anger is what's important, however. It must be channeled for positive action. Ephesians 4:26 says,

"Be angry and do not sin." There is such a thing as righteous anger, though that's probably minimal in our own lives compared to our hurtful behavior when we are angry. When we are angry, we must choose to do something that is not focused on aggression against someone else. Even more resistance can build, and then seeds of bitterness get sown—I have always believed that. Bitterness is the piece that God has not wired us to deal with. If we go down the bitterness road, it's hard to turn around to go back in the other direction. If you let your anger fester, if you swallow your pain, if you let resentment rule, it turns into a nasty pill of bitterness. It's really hard to break free from bitterness in our lives.

Our calling as men is not to hurl rocks but to be solid rocks and walls of protection, conduits of healing to those in our circles of influence. Godly men don't have to justify their masculinity. They simply need to be men, secure and confident.

Surely David had messed up. Instead of seeking God first, he let pride seep in, which led to his self-reliant actions—but I'm quite certain he didn't act alone. Six hundred men rode together in that band. Some of them could have tried to reason with David and encourage him to seek God's will in the matter. Surely some did. Anger was justified, but mutiny was not. There was plenty of blame to go around. Men in general have let their guards down, allowing the enemy to come in. But this is not about blaming. It's about men walking in accountability that leads to action. Ziklag was one of the lowest points for David and his men. They seemed to have lost everything. It appeared as if their lives were in ruins, that life as they knew it was over.

Many men today are disillusioned, depressed, and beaten down. The culture is against them. In some cases their own children are against them or have been turned against them. The temptation is to shift blame, throw stones, or disengage altogether. The truth is that sometimes a man must be brought to a burning Ziklag experience before finally rising up from a place of repentance. Our response after the weeping should not be to pick up stones but to go to God, as David did. When our response is in the spirit of David's, there is a shift that changes everything.

DISCUSSION QUESTIONS

Have you been hurt or betrayed, leaving areas of anger and bitterness in your heart? How so?

Are you blaming God or others for something you should be taking at least partial responsibility for? Why is that the case?

What does it mean to "be angry and do not sin"?

Have you been brought to a burning Ziklag experience? Explain.

SWORD OF THE WORD

Let all bitterness and wrath and anger and clamor and slander
be put away from you, along with all malice.
—EPHESIANS 4:31

PRAY ABOUT IT

Ask the Lord to show you any roots of bitterness in your heart so you can dig them up and get rid of them.

CHAPTER 8

When Evil Is Called Good and Good Is Called Evil

Tolerance is the last virtue of a depraved society. When you have an immoral society that has blatantly, proudly, violated all of the commandments of God, there is one last virtue they insist upon: tolerance for their immorality.

—D. JAMES KENNEDY

IN ANCIENT ISRAEL, when they had no king who represented God's ways, the Bible says, "Everyone did what was right in his own eyes."[1] People became gods to themselves. The result was an overflow of wickedness. As wickedness became the norm, God gave them over to their own desires, which made things even more perverse.[2] He simply turned them over and let them have their way. Psalm 81:11–12 says, "But My people would not heed My voice....So I gave them over to their own stubborn heart, to walk in their own counsels" (NKJV). This is a dangerous place to live. It is a place where people's minds become distorted and they embrace all sorts of perversions and ridiculousness. "Furthermore," Romans 1:28 says, "just as they did not think it worthwhile to retain the knowledge of God, so God gave them over to a depraved mind, so that they do what ought not to be done" (NIV). This is where we are going or even are today as a society—a place where the unthinkable becomes tolerable, then acceptable, then legal, then praised. We are at the point where a man who dares to stand up and be who God created him to be is considered toxic and evil, while a drag queen who reads books to young children and teaches them detestable movements is lauded as brave.[3]

It's getting really bad out there.

Our children are being indoctrinated with anti-God, anti-Christian, anti-family, anti-masculinity rhetoric. The consequences have been dire to say the least. While writing this chapter, I heard about a woman who was explaining Christianity to her precious and sweet granddaughter. "Jesus is dirt!" the granddaughter replied angrily. Really? How does this happen? If I would have responded to my grandmother like that about Jesus, I probably would not have been able to sit down for a bit. That type of attitude was unheard of thirty years ago, yet it's the norm in most of today's high schools and colleges. A militant disrespect for God and Christianity has taken over our schools, entertainment, law, and politics. We have been watching the devastating results unfold right before our eyes—rampant lawlessness, school shootings, godlessness, the feminization and emasculation of men, and things once considered evil being embraced as good, while good from a biblical perspective is labeled as evil. Also, while writing this book, multiple mass shootings took place, including one in a Parkland, Florida, high school; one at a country-western bar in Thousand Oaks, California; one in a Santa Fe, Texas, high school; one in a Pittsburgh synagogue; one in Virginia Beach in a city public works building; one in Dayton, Ohio's Oregon District; and another in a Walmart in El Paso, Texas. Some shootings have involved militant hatred for Christians and even gender-confused individuals. For example, in a school shooting in 2019, in which one person was killed and eight were injured, it was revealed that one of the shooters was gender-confused, and the other posted on social media that he hates Christians.[4]

College and high school students everywhere are being made fun of, humiliated, and even reprimanded for simply believing in two genders, male and female, the way God created them. Case in point: Lake Ingle, a college senior, was kicked out of a class required for graduation simply because he disagreed with his professor's ideology. The disagreement? Ingle believed in two biological genders—male and female, the way God set it up. The feminist professor did not. After showing the class a fifteen-minute TED Talk by a transgender degrading traditional masculinity, the professor asked the students to share their thoughts. Ingle spoke up, challenging his professor's assumption on the basis of biology. He stated that the official view of biologists is that there are only two genders, male and female. But this didn't matter to the professor. Truth and common sense no longer matter. She proceeded to embarrass Ingle before his peers, demanding that he get out of the class and referring him to the public university's Academic Integrity Board. "My professor is violating my First Amendment rights because of the fact that my views and ideology is different from hers," Ingle said. "So she took it on herself to silence and embarrass me—bully me—for speaking up in class."[5]

In a similar case, but this time in a high school, a student was kicked out of class for simply stating there are only two genders, male and female. The headline for the article reads, "Keep Your Beliefs at Home: Student Booted From Class for Saying There Are 2 Genders." The whole conflict, occurring in a detention room, was recorded on video. The student asked why he was being kicked out of class. "You aren't being inclusive," the teacher said. When the student restated his opinion and indicated he was not being discriminatory, the teacher told him to "keep that opinion to your own house and not in this school. I am stating what is national school authority policy." The teacher further stated, "You are saying there is no such thing as anyone other than male or female.... You're making bad choices." At that point, the student asked to be released from detention to go to the research area to resume his classwork, but he was denied.[6]

Recently in Canada, use of the terms *father, mother, sir, madam, Mr.,* and *Mrs.* was banned within a government organization. This was done as an act of tolerance for those with alternate gender identities. Here we see "tolerance" is actually a way to silence or diminish traditional roles. It is not enough to acknowledge those with liberal gender ideas. Traditional gender classifications must be silenced. Government employees were further warned that "the proper use of gender-neutral language will also be added to the observations in the In-Person Quality Monitoring Program."[7] An article notes that "Canada's LGBT industry is one of the most draconian social movements in modern history.... They stop at nothing to get mainstream and heterosexual Canadians to bow to their will."[8] While this is Canada, be assured it's on its way to America. It's a full-frontal attack on biological, biblical definitions of what God said is "good."

A whole book could be filled with cases like these. Sadly it's the new reality of the world in which we live. Bullying and harassment of those who support traditional masculinity have now reached way beyond the classroom, impacting us in every sector—coaches, teachers, fathers, pastors, CEOs, business owners, etc. Every man has to be careful because the PC (political correctness) police are lurking everywhere, waiting to get us for the crime of being too manly. It's all under the guise of tolerance. The truth is they want to make you irrelevant as a man and for you to accept their way of life.

"Years ago, manhood was an opportunity for achievement," wrote Garrison Keillor, "and now it's just a problem to be overcome."[9]

It's difficult enough to stand up for being a traditional biological male. As we've seen, simply stating the obvious can get us in trouble. Go to your local university or high school and stand up and say, "God made me a man, and I'm proud!" and see what happens. You'll likely be shouted down as a bigot and hater. Oh, they will leave us men alone and let us go on our wildlife adventures and to football games as long as we don't try to exert our influence on things that impact the culture, such as our children, especially our boys. Check out this headline: "Court Bars Father From Teaching 6-Year-Old Son That He Is a Boy."[10] This father is still battling to step in and help his son be masculine.[11] Oh, by the way, that one is not in Canada, but good old conservative Texas. Frightening. They want our boys, and to get to them, they must eliminate our influences. They don't want to hear from us men, dads. For the progressive agenda to happen, you have to wipe out real men. If you can wipe out men, you can do anything. Think of it—a father is shamed for wanting to help his son be a boy and could even lose custody of his son because of it. God help us.

DISCUSSION QUESTIONS

What is your understanding of God giving people over to their own stubborn hearts?

How have you been affected by the reports of society's reactions to the belief that there are only two genders, male and female, as God created?

What examples have you seen of good called evil and evil called good?

Are you avoiding the media reporting these aggressions? If so, why?

SWORD OF THE WORD

> Every way of a man is right in his own eyes, but the LORD weighs the heart.
> —PROVERBS 21:2

PRAY ABOUT IT

Pray for God to show you how to best be a godly influence without getting overwhelmed by the negativity.

CHAPTER 9

All-Out War

The fact is, you are going to be assailed. You will have to withstand the onslaughts of the enemy of God. Paul warned us that it would be a rough ride, so fasten your seat belt and focus on your role.

—CHIP INGRAM

AS IF ALL the shaming of traditional men that we've been talking about isn't enough, men who are attempting to live upright, godly lives are being shamed and attacked from another source. They have to daily contend with spiritual forces of darkness coming against them. We've seen that there is a cultural enemy in direct opposition to what we as men are and stand for. This enemy wants society to move on from its Christian heritage to promote its liberal agenda. Behind the scenes of this enemy culture, however, is a very real spiritual force, an actual adversary pulling the strings. Whether you believe it or not, this adversary oversees an entire unseen realm—a hierarchical system that has been in place from the beginning of time, with the sole intent of disrupting God's plan. Of course the scientific culture of the day scoffs at such a notion. If you can't see it with your natural eyes, then it doesn't exist. As Christians, however, we know better. Jesus Himself believed in a literal adversary. When the Spirit of God led Jesus into the wilderness before His ministry began, the Bible says He was tempted by the devil. Each time Jesus was tempted, He replied directly to the person of Satan. Jesus wasn't talking to some metaphysical force or allegorical figure. He was addressing an actual entity that exists in another realm, the leader of the hosts of darkness. Matthew 4:10 says, "Jesus said to him, 'Away with you, Satan! For it is written, "You shall worship the LORD your God"'" (NKJV). The next verse says, "Then the devil left Him, and behold, angels came and ministered to Him."[1] A war is going on in the spiritual realm that affects the physical. As men, it is essential for us to know this so we can better understand how to fight.

C. S. Lewis wrote, "There are two equal and opposite errors into which our race can fall about the devils. One is to disbelieve in their existence. The other is to believe, and to feel an excessive and unhealthy interest in them."[2] Charles Spurgeon warned that Satan "has studied mankind very thoroughly, and knows all our weak points. Therefore, the contest will be an unequal one. Do not argue with him but wave in his face the banner of God's Word."[3] That's what Jesus did. The apostle Paul affirmed that is what we should do also "in order that Satan might not outwit us. For we are not unaware of his schemes."[4] Paul further notes that "we do not wrestle against flesh and blood, but against principalities, against powers, against the rulers of the darkness of this age, against spiritual hosts of wickedness in the heavenly places."[5]

Later on we will delve into the ins and outs of spiritual warfare, but for now I simply want to show that we have a very real adversary that has schemes and literal forces behind those schemes to execute them. One of Satan's major schemes is to bring down men. It's a strategic, spiritual attack on biblical masculinity.

These very real principalities and powers are working in conjunction with a man's own flesh, which is endlessly being enticed by our overly sensual, fallen world. The struggle to be a godly man in today's society is brutal. It is an all-out war. C. S. Lewis wrote, "Only those who try to resist temptation know how strong it is. After all, you find out the strength of the German army by fighting against it, not by giving in. You find out the strength of a wind by trying to walk against it, not by lying down."[6] Godly men are fighting not only a culture that's against their masculinity and manhood but also the temptations and spiritual tensions of this world set on bringing them down. Toss into the mix stress, fatigue, financial expectations to perform, pressures to be unethical, time demands, and loneliness—not to mention pornographic images pounding them relentlessly from a myriad of sources. These are only some of the issues that godly men wrestle with on a regular basis.

Dangling on the Ropes or Comatose

Though many men may be striving to please God, they are living in perpetual defeat as a result of this onslaught from all sides. Weary, worn, and broken down, some are dangling on the ropes. Some have been knocked to the canvas. When they try to stand up and be the men they long to be, they get shoved back down. "Shut up and stay put!" the culture and the accuser of the brethren shout. "Nobody cares what you think. You're not good enough. God's mad at you. You don't make a difference. You'll never win. Just stay down!" Other men are slumped in the corner, contemplating whether it's even worth it to get back in the fight. "Do I want it?" they are asking themselves. "Do I really want the things of God? Is it worth the fight, the struggle? Does it really matter? Do I really matter?" Still others have been pounded into a comatose state or are sitting on the stool in the corner with their heads hung low. Living lives of secret despair, they feel ashamed and overwhelmed, and they think it is too late for them. They are convinced they will never be free.

If you are one of those who feel sucker punched, discouraged, and down and out, take heart. It's not too late! God wants you. He's not finished with you. In fact your best days as a man lie ahead. "Falling down is how we grow," decreed Maximus in the movie *Gladiator*. "Staying down is how we die."[7] One of the purposes of this book is to encourage men who are down, who are on the verge of giving up, or who have given up to get back up! You're not alone!

An Uprising

Just as there was a stirring in George Foreman and in King David to rise up and take on the giants in their lives, a stirring is going on in the hearts of men all across our land. It's a battle call, prompted by the Holy Spirit. God is rallying His troops. And guess what?

Men are heeding the call and reporting to duty.

You can feel it in the air, a rumble in the distance like thunder rolling in.

It's an army of men who are fed up with being beaten up by those who want to feminize and emasculate them. They are tired of living lives of compromise and sin, and the battle lines have been drawn. Men are stepping back into the ring. This time, as with George, they are fighting for something bigger than themselves. Nehemiah 4:14 is their banner: "Do not be afraid of them. Remember the Lord, great and awesome, and fight for your brethren, your sons, your daughters, your wives, and your houses" (NKJV). Psalm 144:1 is their decree: "Blessed be the LORD my Rock, who trains my hands for war, and my fingers for battle" (NKJV). But these guys know that for them to succeed, it has to be a God thing. They can't do it in their own strength.

Yes, a storm cloud is rolling in. It's a storm cloud of men.

Richard J. Foster wrote, "In our day heaven and earth are on tiptoe waiting for the emerging of a Spirit-led, Spirit-intoxicated, Spirit-empowered people."[8] I would add heaven and earth are on tiptoe awaiting Spirit-led, Spirit-intoxicated men, brothers, servants, followers of Christ who are willing to stand in the gap for such a time as this.

It's an uprising.

Lightning is about to strike!

DISCUSSION QUESTIONS

Are you going along with life as usual, avoiding controversial issues; or are you struggling against the enemy's attacks? Why or why not?

Have you recognized some schemes of the enemy in your life? Explain.

Are you wrestling with the onslaught of our overly sensual, fallen world? How so?

SWORD OF THE WORD

Remember the Lord, who is great and awesome, and fight for your brothers, your sons, your daughters, your wives, and your homes.

—NEHEMIAH 4:14

PRAY ABOUT IT

If you're feeling defeated and knocked down, pray for God to lift you up and fortify you for the work He has for you.

CHAPTER 10

Purposefully Designed

Stand true to your calling to be a man. Real
women will always be relieved and grateful
when men are willing to be men.

—ELISABETH ELLIOT

AN INTERNATIONAL SPACE exploration research team conducted a study on the possible colonization of Mars. When the findings were presented to NASA, the study suggested that "all-female astronaut crews could reproduce in space without the help of accompanying men." The study concluded that frozen sperm samples exposed to simulations of weightlessness in space maintained the same characteristics as sperm on the ground with gravity. This raised "hopes that a sperm bank could one day be set up in space to help populate new worlds." It also meant that future missions to Mars could consist of female-only space crews.[1]

This study was met with great fanfare, especially among feminist and anti-masculinity groups. In response to the female-only astronaut crews, one individual wrote, "But who's going to kill the spiders on the ship?" My wife, Julie, would have said, "It sure won't be Tim!" Obviously someone was trying to add some humor to the dialogue, but there's an element of the statement that rings true in our cores. Men are good at killing bugs, along with doing a lot of other meaningful tasks. God created men for a reason—not just for their sperm.

Specific Roles

The world was built on the backs of strong men. I can just feel all the women out there cringing. When statements such as "Men built this society" are made, one almost feels the need to apologize. Surely someone is going to be offended: "That's so biased and bigoted. It's chauvinistic." Yet it is not meant to be sexist or misogynistic. We are not saying that women can't kill spiders and do all sorts of things that men can do. They certainly can, and they do. Men are not better than women. They are certainly not smarter! This book is not meant to minimize women in any way. We need strong, godly women in the fight too. Men can't survive without them and what they bring to the table. We are elevating their gifts. But it's unreasonable to say men and women are the same. They are equal, but they are not the same. To not recognize this is to throw common sense out the window. Women are strong emotionally, physically, and spiritually, just in a different way than men. If men had to go through labor pains, society would have died off years ago! No, women are very strong—in some ways stronger than men. But this book is about men and why men matter. Men, it's OK to embrace how God made you.

Both men and women are equally unique, each reflecting the image of God in their own way. "So God created mankind in his own image, in the image of God he created them; male and female he created them."[2] God purposefully designed men and women the way they are, and that is a good thing. He said so Himself. "Then God saw everything that He had made, and indeed it was very good."[3]

The most obvious purpose for our differences is the procreation of the human species. Without our biological distinctions the species would die off. However, our distinctiveness goes much further than that, into our God-given instincts, ways of thinking, gifts, and roles. Man was made to complement woman, and woman was made to complement man. Now, you may be reading this and thinking, "Duh." All of it may seem extremely elementary. And it *is* extremely elementary, except that the forces against us are set on blurring these common-sense, natural lines of creation. In California, for example, the legislature passed the Gender Recognition Act, allowing for a third, nonbinary gender category on driver's licenses and other state-issued identification. Other states have followed suit. State Senator Hannah-Beth Jackson said, "We are now a state recognizing the nonbinary designation as a gender."[4] In other words, and I'm paraphrasing, "We don't accept the natural two-gender order, male and female, the way God created them. There are more genders, and we must not offend them."

Please understand. This book is not intended as an attack on individuals who struggle with their sexual identity. Rather, it is about the way God-defined masculinity is being undermined and what we can do about it. Those who want to deny or confuse the inherent, biological order and biblical roles do so in an effort to normalize an unnatural worldview. In fact, since the Garden of Eden, one of Satan's goals has been to pervert or blur what God called good. The great evangelist Billy Sunday said, "No one can read the Bible in a thoughtful way without being impressed with the fact that it makes much of manhood, and holds it up as something that should be sought after with diligence and perseverance. In fact the Bible exalts and emphasizes manhood in a remarkable way, and shows that real manhood is a great thing in the world."[5]

Our culture, however, is being indoctrinated to believe that our God-given roles are narrow and restrictive, bigoted, or hateful. On the contrary, to embrace God's order is a good thing, bringing about ultimate freedom for both men and women. Thank God for all the women heroes who have displayed unshakable courage. For some it was out of necessity because men in their lives dropped the ball. The world desperately needs the gifts and insights that only women can bring. They are critical to the equation, and godly women need to rise up too and fully embrace their womanhood.

Nonetheless the fact remains that men *are* difference makers. Without masculine men everything falls into disorder, leaving gaping holes for the enemy to occupy.

DISCUSSION QUESTIONS

In what ways do you feel like you matter as a man?

How is traditional masculinity coming under attack in your life?

Who are the godly women God has put in your life over the years, and what do they mean to you?

SWORD OF THE WORD

Be watchful, stand firm in the faith, act like men, be strong.
—1 Corinthians 16:13

PRAY ABOUT IT

If you're wondering why it's such a big deal to defend the God-ordained genders for men and women, pray for God to open the eyes of your understanding to grasp its importance based on the Word of God.

CHAPTER 11

The Difference Makers

In a sort of ghastly simplicity we remove the organ and demand the function. We make men without chests and expect of them virtue and enterprise. We laugh at honour and are shocked to find traitors in our midst. We castrate and bid the geldings be fruitful.

—C. S. LEWIS

YES, MEN ARE rising up. But I'm warning you, the enemy and those under his influence aren't taking it lying down! They are rising up too, and their heels are dug in. It's going to be a lights-out, winner-take-all brawl. But why so much fuss and fighting against men and traditional masculinity? It's because the enemy knows if he can take down men and their masculinity, he wins. That's why there's a big target on you. If you have any value to God, I believe all hell will be against you. And that's why, regardless of where you are in life, it's more important than ever for you to rise up and be the man God created you to be.

You matter that much.

The Stats That Blew Me Away

While doing research for this book, I came across some stats about men that blew me away! They really set the precedent for the rest of this book. According to Promise Keepers at Work, when a father attends church, there's a 93 percent chance that everyone else in the household will too.[1] That is not a misprint—93 percent! Let that sink in for a moment. That's a staggering statistic.

This clearly demonstrates that men matter because when you take them out of the equation, the figure plummets. A survey in Switzerland shows if the father does *not* attend church, even if the mother is a regular attender, only about one child in sixty-six will become a regular church attender. If the dad is an irregular attender and the mom is a regular attender, approximately one in twenty-nine children will become a regular church attender. But if both the mom and the dad are regular attenders, about one in three children will become regular church attenders.[2] That is huge! It is not just about sporadic church attendance; regular attendance can make a huge difference. Promise Keepers reported that if a child is the first one in the household to attend church, there is only a 3.5 percent probability that the rest of the family will follow. If the mother is the first to attend church, there is only a 17 percent probability that her family will attend too. But remember, with Dad it's 93 percent.[3]

In his book *Families and Faith: How Religion Is Passed Down Across Generations*, University of Southern California research professor Vern Bengtson also showed how critical dads are when it comes to issues of faith. He focused on close relationships between fathers and their children and the spiritual power this exerts on their lives. According to Bengtson, 68 percent of children who have a strong relationship with their fathers will continue their fathers' level of religious participation. Only 30 percent of those having weaker relationships with their fathers continue their fathers' level of religious participation.[4]

All the statistics are similar and send a strong message: when it comes to issues of faith, men don't just matter—they are critical.

"When a man lives up to his role, life-giving things start to happen," wrote Rod Hairston. "I firmly believe that every family and societal problem can get better when a man knows how to fulfill his role and takes action.... In life, we men cannot afford to blow our assignments. It's not merely a team that is counting on us; it's all of society."[5]

I recently heard the story of a man who pastored a successful church for over forty years, impacting thousands of lives for Christ. While he was growing up, his father was a bitter alcoholic, and the family was in chaos. One day the father was invited to church by a man he worked with and for some odd reason said, "Why not?" He didn't go alone but brought the whole family with him. At church that Sunday morning, the conviction of God fell on him. When Communion was offered, he refused, feeling unworthy. The pastor called for prayer up front. When he did, the father stood up and ran to the altar for prayer, after which he made a public profession of faith before the congregation. Right there, everyone else in the family followed to the altar—brother, sisters, and mother. The whole family got saved that day, and a great healing took place. Now, imagine for a moment what would have happened to that family if the father had not had the guts to stand up and make that change? Who knows? But because he did, one family was resurrected—not to mention that his son became a pastor. Think of the power of that.

Stories such as this one, along with the statistics, show that men are meant to be leaders and that they wield powerful influence. A man's faith impacts those around him. Children follow their fathers. And every man has a circle of influence, even if that circle is small. You cannot *not* have influence—good or bad!

Children whose fathers are involved in their lives are 70 percent less likely to drop out of school.[6] Children with fathers involved in their schools are as much as 43 percent more likely to get A's in school.[7] Even in high-crime neighborhoods, 90 percent of children from stable homes with both a father and a mother do not become delinquents.[8] Statistics show that adolescent girls with involved fathers are significantly less likely to be sexually active than when the father is absent. Meg Meeker noted in her book *Strong Fathers, Strong Daughters* that "76 percent of teen girls said that fathers influenced their decisions [for good or bad] on whether they should become sexually active."[9] Unfortunately, if a father is not a man of God, chances are his family will follow him—into immorality, into atheism, and in the way he treats women and his wife. When Dad is out of the picture, either physically or emotionally, it's not good. It leaves a gaping, empty hole in our kids that the enemy has rushed in to fill with counterfeits and lies. While these sobering statistics are not new to most of us, they don't lie.

- 85 percent of all children who show behavior disorders come from fatherless homes.

- 85 percent of rapists motivated by displaced anger problems come from fatherless homes.

- 70 percent of youths in state-operated institutions come from fatherless homes.

- 75 percent of all adolescent patients in substance abuse facilities come from fatherless homes.

- 71 percent of all high school dropouts come from fatherless homes.[10]

- 90 percent of all homeless and runaway children are from fatherless homes.

- 70 percent of all juveniles in correctional facilities come from fatherless homes.

- 70 percent of pregnant teenagers lack father involvement.[11]

A 2009 survey by the National Center for Fathering revealed that seven out of ten people "agree that the physical absence of fathers from the home is the most significant family or social problem facing America." The same survey also revealed that only half of respondents "give most fathers credit for knowing what is going on in their children's lives."[12]

Here's more sobering information: in school shootings boys are overwhelmingly the ones pulling the triggers, not girls. So many of the shooters listed in CNN's "Mass Shootings in the US Fast Facts" were boys or young men.[13] But here's the real kicker: the vast majority of them were *fatherless*. A 2013 article by W. Bradford Wilcox, senior fellow at the Institute for Family Studies, noted that "one common and largely unremarked thread tying together most of the school shooters that have struck the nation in the last year is that they came from homes marked by divorce or an absent father."[14] A more recent (2018) investigation of twenty-seven mass shooters led to the same conclusion.[15]

Who knows how many lives would have been saved if some dads would have stepped up in those boys' lives before the shootings? To say that men are significant is an understatement. They matter. They have a distinct impact both positively and negatively. John J. Smithbaker wrote in an overview of his book *The Great American Rescue Mission: Reaching and Healing the Fatherless*:

> Angry, lost, wounded and emotionally crippled boys are more dangerous to themselves and others. They carry those wounds forward and fail to develop into the men that God designed and America needs to be a strong and healthy nation....Generational fatherlessness is eroding the

foundation of the family—society's backbone.... [America] is a nation worth defending. That's why we desperately need the next generation of pastors, providers and protectors to WIN this soul crushing battle for our families, our children and our country.[16]

Single Men With Father Spirits

While these statistics are primarily about fathers, masculinity and fatherhood are invariably linked. That's because you can't talk about real manhood without talking about fatherhood. Every man has a biological father who impacted him positively or negatively. Suzanne Venker of Fox News said, "The root of fatherlessness is deep and wide, but it ultimately rests in two things: our culture's dismissal of men as valuable human beings who have something unique to offer—on the one hand, we tell them to 'man up,' and on the other we tell them manhood is the problem—and its dismissal of marriage as an institution that's crucial to the health and well-being of children."[17]

Regardless of what type of father you had, men and their masculinity are valuable, especially when in God's hands. Every man, whether he is a father or not, can have a father spirit and impact those around him. George Foreman grew up with an absentee father. As a result he wound up a rebellious delinquent on the run from the police.[18] Thankfully, real men rose up and stepped into George's life to help turn him in the right direction. "I came in contact with some real men with integrity who showed a genuine interest in me," George said. "They had within them the ingredients of authority, life experience, and love.... They were men who I could look up to, men I was motivated to please and emulate.... I don't know where I would have ended up if not for men like [that]."[19]

Today, we need men like these to rise up and embrace the way God created them, to get involved and make a difference. The foundation of America is depending on it. We do it one person, one circle of influence, at a time. Every man has an influence. In the foreword to Pastor Larry Stockstill's *Model Man*, Pastor Chris Hodges wrote, "Behind every great man is a great...*man*."[20] This is true. Is it any wonder that the enemy of all enemies wants men out of the picture?

Here's the simple equation: breakdown of men = breakdown of family and circles of influence (job, team, school, family, church, etc.) = breakdown of a nation and culture.

Being a man and being masculine is good. It's that simple. Everything hinges on men—really everything. Without strong, masculine men, the culture falls apart.

For good or bad, positive or negative, men matter.

You matter.

Will you be a difference maker for good? If you have blown it, keep reading. God is for you. He wants you back in the fight.

DISCUSSION QUESTIONS

Are you questioning whether you matter as a man? Does your life count? Why?

Are there areas in your life where you're experiencing divine tension? Explain.

How can you fulfill your role as a man and take action?

What men in your life have impacted you with a father spirit and motivated you to embrace God's role for you?

SWORD OF THE WORD

Give justice to the weak and the fatherless.

—PSALM 82:3

PRAY ABOUT IT

Pray for the Lord to give you a father spirit to help combat the epidemic of fatherlessness in our society. Ask Him how you can be father to the fatherless.

CHAPTER 12

Flip the Script

Nations that are populated largely by
immature, immoral, weak-willed, cowardly, and
self-indulgent men cannot and will not long endure.

—JAMES DOBSON

ON JANUARY 1, 1929, the California Golden Bears played the Georgia Tech Yellow Jackets in the Rose Bowl in Pasadena, California. Early in the second quarter, before more than sixty-six thousand screaming fans, California's Roy Riegels scooped up a Georgia Tech fumble and began running like an Olympic sprinter toward the goal line. There was only one problem: Riegels ran sixty-nine yards in the wrong direction! Finally he was taken down by one of his own teammates at the one-yard line. Riegels was so upset and humiliated by his mistake that he felt there was no way he could show his face before the crowd, much less play another down. On the bench all he could do was hang his head in shame.

During halftime in the locker room it was announced that everyone who started the first half would be starting the second half, but when the rest of his team headed back out on the field, Riegels remained where he was. He said, "Coach, I can't do it. I've ruined you. I've ruined my school. I've ruined myself. I couldn't face the crowd in that stadium to save my life."

"Roy, get up and go back," his coach ordered. "The game is only half over!"[1]

Ashamed and distraught yet urged on by his coach and teammates, Riegels somehow willed himself back in the game. Not only did he play again, but he turned in an all-star performance, even blocking a Georgia Tech punt. Unfortunately it wasn't enough. Georgia Tech wound up winning 8 to 7. Riegels' blunder had cost the game, and he was tagged "Wrong Way" Riegels for life. The great news in this story is that Riegels did not let that negative label define him. In fact he flipped the script and turned it into a positive that made him a better man. He wound up a first-team All-American, was voted team captain in 1929, and was voted into the Rose Bowl Hall of Fame. His coach, Nibs Price, said Roy Riegels "was the smartest player [he] ever coached."[2] Riegels went on to serve as a major in the United States Army Air Corps in World War II. After the war he became a successful businessman, and motivational speakers have used his story as an example of overcoming mistakes.

Just like with Roy Riegels, there are many unflattering labels on men that cause us to hang our heads in shame. We just saw a few of the devastating effects when men are absent, but there's much more to the problem than simply not showing up. Men have been running in the wrong direction for too long.

- While it is hard to get accurate figures for the number of married men who have cheated on their wives, a 2010–2016 survey reported that 20 percent of husbands have affairs, with higher percentages among older married men.[3]

- A survey reported that 74 percent of all married men said they would have an affair if they would never get caught.[4]

- A 2016 Barna study reported that 64 percent of Christian men view pornography at least once a month, and 21 percent say they are addicted. One in five youth pastors and one in seven senior pastors use pornography regularly.[5]

- According to a 2009 study by the Josephson Institute of Ethics, 51 percent of teenagers 17 and under believe that lying and cheating are necessary to succeed. This shift in attitude has been particularly strong among young men,[6] rendering them less likely (and able) to live up to God's call to honesty and integrity.

- According to an article in *Psychology Today*, "Men are overwhelmingly represented in several diagnostic categories, sometimes called 'impulse control disorders'—predilections that lead to alcohol and drug abuse, sexual misbehaviors of various kinds, violent outbursts, delinquency, problems holding down a job, and an overrepresentation in almost all categories of criminal activity (with consequent overrepresentation in arrest records and prison terms)....They're also more likely to steal, cheat, and engage in various criminal activities for money (from small-time drug dealers to big-time Wall Street swindlers...)."[7]

I could go on and on and on. But I want to make this point crystal clear. These aren't merely stats and disorders. Much of it is also sin.

Men are in deep trouble with sin. And sin doesn't just destroy our own souls. It destroys our relationships, our families, and the souls of the ones we love most. When we don't step up and turn away from ungodliness, sin rules us, and the consequences are frightening.

As men we have to do better. Let's face it. Women are not the problem. We are. James Dobson summed it up well when he wrote, "Nations that are populated largely by immature, immoral, weak-willed, cowardly, and self-indulgent men cannot and will not long endure. These types of men include those who sire and abandon their children; who cheat on the ones they love; who lie, steal, and covet; who hate their countrymen; and who serve no god but money. That is the direction culture is taking today's boys."[8] Jesus couldn't have been any plainer when He stated, "For from within, out of the heart of men, proceed evil thoughts, adulteries, fornications, murders, thefts, covetousness, wickedness, deceit, lewdness, an evil eye, blasphemy, pride, foolishness. All these evil things come from within and defile a man."[9]

Men, we need to get the smelling salts out and wake up from our comas!

We need to let go of the shame because of our screwups, get back in the game, and play our hearts out!

Toxic Behavior Versus Toxic Masculinity

No doubt, a man's behavior can be toxic, or sinful, if you want to put it another way. But so can a woman's behavior. Society's answer to this dilemma, therefore, has been to label masculinity as toxic and to emasculate and feminize us. Justin Trudeau, the prime minister of Canada, said that he is raising his children, including his two sons, as feminists "to change our culture of sexism."[10] This solution does not work. Instead it's destroying men. While the behavior of some (not all) men is toxic, their masculinity is not. The negative stats in the last two chapters don't paint the whole picture. Men can change—and are changing—by the power of God. And that starts by dealing with our sin problem.

Make no mistake about it—there is a culture of sexism and toxic behavior, even in the church. Women have been experiencing hurtful behavior by men for years. My wife Julie has been hosting the Extraordinary Women Conferences for years, and we've heard from a lot of women about the abuses and objectifying that they've encountered from men. Again, this behavior from men is sin. I must point out here that we also hear from women who have deep appreciation of those solid, godly men who do not fall into this category, who show respect and honor to women.

If you are reading this and feel a sense of injustice to women, that's the Spirit of God rising up in you. Jesus treated women with dignity and respect. The Word of God commands it.

The good news is, men, you have a choice. You do not have to be ruled by toxic behavior, which is sin. Your masculinity is not sinful; it is good. Embrace it. The strength that can be used to mistreat women is the same strength and power that can be used to protect them, stand up for them (when you see wrongdoing by other males), and cherish them. Harness your masculinity for good. Strength under control is a strength that can be used for good. Just as Roy Riegels didn't let his wrong-way run ultimately define him, negative labels and statistics do not have to define what a man is or what a man can become—even if he has messed up or has exhibited toxic behavior.

Not Toxic, Not Better, but Godly

As stated above, the world's remedy to toxic behavior is the emasculation and feminization of men. Michael Ian Black, in an op-ed for the *New York Times*, wrote, "There has to be a way to expand what it means to be a man without losing our masculinity."[11] Black is right.

There is a way. Allie Stuckey of PragerU almost got it right when she said, "The answer to toxic masculinity isn't less masculinity; it's better masculinity."[12] We say the answer isn't better masculinity or, honestly, even traditional masculinity but *godly* masculinity.

After God created both male and female and deemed them good, sin entered the world, corrupting our natures. All of us are bent toward sin. Men, even traditional men, can't be better on their own. Only by living through the power of the Holy Spirit can a man fulfill the purpose for which he was designed. Without the Spirit of God working in us, we are going to exhibit toxic behavior because we live in a fallen, sinful world and we have a sin nature. The apostle Paul wrote in Romans 7:18, "For I know that nothing good dwells in me, that is, in my flesh." Though his spirit man was perfect and born again, Paul still had his flesh to deal with. So does every man. The good news is the Christian man has the Holy Spirit within him. God's answer to toxic masculinity is men filled with His Spirit. The Scripture says that Jesus is the vine and we are the branches. When we abide in the vine (Jesus), we will bear much fruit, and apart from Him we can do nothing.[13] Abide in Jesus, and we bear much fruit. Do not abide, and our flesh rules. Galatians 5:22–23 says, "But the fruit of the Spirit is love, joy, peace, patience, kindness, goodness, faithfulness, gentleness, self-control; against such things there is no law." The fruit of the Spirit is the exact opposite of the toxic behavior many men exhibit and, I dare to say, encompasses the qualities most women want from men and what society needs from men. The way it happens, however, is not through emasculation but through the Holy Spirit's control. This type of manhood is the key to turning this thing around—godly men fulfilling their masculine roles by the power of the Holy Spirit, the Spirit of Christ, coming alive in them and bearing fruit.

Men, we have a choice. We can give in to sin and toxic behavior, or we can embrace righteousness. We can stay on the bench after our screwups with our heads hung in shame, or we can rise up, get back in the game, and let God flip the script of our lives.

DISCUSSION QUESTIONS

Have you been running in the wrong direction? Explain.

Are you treating the women in your life with dignity and respect? What are some areas you could improve in?

Are you fulfilling the purpose to which God designed you through the power of the Holy Spirit? Why or why not?

SWORD OF THE WORD

> But the fruit of the Spirit is love, joy, peace, patience, kindness, goodness, faithfulness, gentleness, self-control; against such things there is no law.
>
> —GALATIANS 5:22–23

PRAY ABOUT IT

Be honest with yourself and open yourself up to the light of the Holy Spirit. If you found yourself reflected in some of the negative statistics discussed, call it what it is—sin. Repent and ask God to forgive and cleanse you.

CHAPTER 13

Sheba: A Worthless Man

I love being a man. I don't feel ashamed,
embarrassed, intimidated or guilty about it. But I
know I'm not what I shall be. I am what I am, and I'm
more than I was. But I'm not all the man I can be.
—EDWIN LOUIS COLE

WHAT DOES IT really mean to be a man? Not someone labeled as toxic, traditional, conservative, or even religious. Not just someone with male anatomy. You can be any or all of those things and not be the man God wants or created you to be.

You can be buff and tough and miss the mark of true manhood. You could be a Sheba. What's a Sheba? A Sheba is a worthless man, and that's one thing you never want to be called. It's a male who wastes his masculinity by not letting God use it. It comes straight from the Bible. "Now there happened to be there a worthless man, whose name was Sheba, the son of Bichri, a Benjaminite. And he blew the trumpet and said, 'We have no portion in David, and we have no inheritance in the son of Jesse; every man to his tents, O Israel!'"[1] The actual Hebrew word for a *worthless man* in this passage is *bĕliya'al,* and it means a worthless man, a troublemaker, ungodly.[2] This guy Sheba was worthless, but he thought he was really something. An arrogant, loudmouthed know-it-all, he blew his trumpet against God's plan. With a heart of rebellion and unbelief he was sure that he knew more than anyone else. In actuality he was a nobody, throwing a wet blanket on what God was doing through King David. I like the way the Living Bible puts it: "Then a hothead whose name was Sheba (son of Bichri, a Benjaminite) blew a trumpet and yelled, 'We want nothing to do with David. Come on, you men of Israel, let's get out of here. He's not our king!'" How many of us can relate to someone like that?

It's called rebellion and disobedience. But that wasn't all.

Notice the next verse: "So all *except* Judah and Benjamin turned around and deserted David and followed Sheba! *But* the men of Judah stayed with their king, accompanying him from the Jordan to Jerusalem."[3] I don't know about you, but I want to be in the "except" and "but" categories of men when it comes to the things of God. Those guys who stood with King David were committed to God's plan by faith. And in the end they were rewarded. They accompanied David when he moved into Jerusalem to assume his reign. Sheba, on the other hand, was executed along with many of his followers. Here's a warning: be careful whom you listen to and even more careful whom you follow. "See to it that no one takes you captive by philosophy and empty deceit," Paul wrote, "according to human tradition, according to the elemental spirits of the world, and not according to Christ."[4] *Elemental spirits* are worldly thinking and deceptive arguments. Shebas weave a web of logic mixed with just enough misinformation to distort the truth and promote what the people want to hear and believe. They're always trying to shut down God's men, because Shebas are ruled by fear and insecurity that manifests through false masculinity and toxic behavior. The modern-day term for Sheba is someone who chokes under pressure, someone who bails, someone who can't take the heat when put to the test. We don't want to be like that. We don't want to be chokers. In sports the one word you don't want to be labeled with is *choker*. In life you don't want to be labeled as a choker either.

Following David wasn't always safe. It took fighters to follow David—those who could discern the situation and follow the right path in spite of the difficulties.

The army of men that God is calling to rise up, those whom heaven and earth are standing on tiptoes for, aren't just any men. They certainly aren't Shebas. They boldly declare who they are but not as loudmouthed know-it-alls. "In quietness and confidence," wrote Isaiah, "shall be your strength."[5] Covered with God's quiet confidence, they work to be strong and solid, knowing how to love, serve, and respect women. They aren't climbing back into the ring, swinging at air and throwing wild punches. No, their gloves are fastened tight with the truth of God, and their feet are firmly planted in His Word. In the same way that George Foreman quietly and confidently faced his critics and surged ahead with God's plan for his life, these men are surging forward in the face of their critics. They've taken their punches and are pillars of truth standing firm for God's best, fully embracing His definition of manhood.

We're seeing it at our conferences and events: men flocking to the altar, hungry, broken, sick and tired of sin, crying out for change—change in their own lives, change in their families, and change in their nation. We get cards and letters, thousands of them, from men desperate for more of God so they can become conduits of change in our crumbling culture. Here's a sample:

> I grew up in a drug-dealing home, and I fell in that lifestyle. I was lost and felt I had no purpose. Later my mom died of an overdose, and right when I needed Jesus, He showed up in my life. I have been delivered from that lifestyle now. I'm married with kids, but I feel I am at a standstill in my walk and need the fire back and God's purpose in my life.

—James

I want my pride to get out of the way and let Him operate in love through me. I want to be a true, dedicated servant, to go beyond knowledge and take action to glorify my Creator.

—Greg

Lord, forgive me. I have held hatred in my heart for my earthly father for things he has done to me. Father, please forgive me and give me the strength and power to forgive him and be the light to the world that You have called me to be.

—Fred

Make me a better father and husband. I surrender all to you, Lord. Search my heart for any wickedness. Change my ways of thinking.

—Marcus

I want to be a better dad and show my daughter every day how much she means to me. I want to be a better son and a better disciple of Your Word.

—Dale

Please bring me closer to You, Lord, and make me a more godly man to my family. I want to live my life in You, Lord. Please help me.

—Jeremy

Forgive me, God. I need You to make me the man that You made me to be.

—Gabe

These wounded warriors, and the thousands like them, are a dangerous force to be reckoned with. They recognize that staying down on the canvas or slumped in their corners is not a solution to the onslaught they're facing. They want their voices back—not so they can flex their muscles, not for their own glory, but so they can make a difference for good. They don't want to taunt their foes but to kneel in the corner giving glory to God. These guys don't want to just be male or masculine. They want to be examples—patterns of godly manhood that can be followed.

They are like King Josiah who, despite his young age, changed the course of a nation. In 2 Kings 23:3 it says that Josiah "made a covenant before the LORD, to walk after the LORD and to keep his commandments." Even though he was a young king, Josiah was a man of character and integrity, willing to stand up for what was good and to expose evil. This is the type of man needed in the army rising up—men called to holiness, to boldness; men called to love and be loved; those who would separate themselves from the pack. The Bible says more about Josiah: "Before him there was no king like him, who turned to the LORD with all his heart and with all his soul and with all his might, according to all the Law of Moses, nor did any like him arise after him."[6]

You get that? Josiah "turned to the LORD with all his heart and with all his soul and with all his might." He wasn't divided in his heart. He wasn't divided in his soul. He wasn't divided in his commitment. We need undivided men, wholly committed to the cause. We need men who have turned to the Lord and are following hard after Him.

Sometimes a man needs to turn. Is it time for you to turn?

You can be any age—young or old—and have the heart of a Josiah, not a Sheba. You can be any age and turn toward the Lord with all your heart. As long as God has given you breath, there's still a battle to fight. There is still something for you to do, something for you to redeem, to conquer, to reclaim. That's your calling as a man.

Don't sit around and be a worthless man. Get up and make a difference! Make a covenant with the Lord and be a dangerous force for the enemy to reckon with. Exhibit godly masculinity, holiness, and boldness. Be separate from the pack.

DISCUSSION QUESTIONS

Is your heart in obedience to God and committed to following His plan? Explain.

What can you do to prepare yourself to not choke under pressure?

How can you be a man filled with quiet confidence?

SWORD OF THE WORD

In quietness and confidence shall be your strength.
—ISAIAH 30:15, NKJV

PRAY ABOUT IT

Ask God to fill you with His Holy Spirit so that you may be set apart for Him, holy, blameless, confident, and bold.

CHAPTER 14
Get Dialed In

Men, in a word, must necessarily be controlled, either
by a power within them, or by a power without
them; either by the word of God, or by the strong
arm of man; either by the Bible, or by the bayonet.
—ROBERT C. WINTHROP

WHEN SOMEONE IS dialed in, it means that person has a clear line. The static has been eliminated. With cell phones, getting dialed in is the equivalent of getting a clear signal instead of it breaking up. Sometimes events happen in our lives that cause static or broken signals. We are living life, but things are out of sync. We aren't performing well. In sports, when you are out of sync, when your shot is off, you get back in the gym alone and practice that jump shot or you get back to the foul line and shoot free throws to get dialed in. When you are in a slump at the plate, you get back into the batter's cage. You go back to the basics, back to the fundamentals, to get yourself anchored. These days there's so much parity in professional sports that the majority of the time a game is won or lost because of a breakdown in the fundamentals. This is why even at a professional level great athletes spend hours and hours working on fundamentals. Drew Brees, the future Hall of Famer, still spends hours upon hours working on his footwork and delivery. The great

Michael Jordan shined like no one else in game-time situations. He won six NBA championships, was the NBA Finals MVP six times, was the NBA's Most Valuable Player five times, and was an NBA All-Star fourteen times. Jordan warns, "The minute you get away from the fundamentals—whether it's proper technique, work ethic, or mental preparation—the bottom can fall out of your game, your schoolwork, your job, whatever you're doing."[1] Getting back to the fundamentals of your game is like getting rid of the static or getting back into position to receive a clear signal.

Going back to the story of Ziklag, David was in trouble. His men were talking about stoning him because of what had happened to their wives and children. But at a point where many men would sink into a deep pit of depression or even consider suicide, David got dialed in. He turned back to the fundamentals, back to his true source of strength, and got in position to receive a clear signal. He wept again, but instead of cries of grief, he cried out to his God: "David was greatly distressed.... But David strengthened himself in the LORD his God."[2] Although David was feeling the same trauma as his men, the shepherd-warrior future king fell back on his roots. Yes, he had made some serious mistakes and led his men down an ill-chosen path. But David knew to whom he belonged, and he knew God was the only One who could help him. David didn't cry out to just any god. He cried out to *his* God, the God of Abraham, Isaac, and Jacob. Although he was devastated, defeated, and disliked at that moment, David knew where his source of empowerment lay.

Alone, perhaps in a cave or on a hilltop overlooking the Promised Land, David surely recalled how God had come through for him again and again. Years before, while David was shepherding sheep, God had delivered him out of the jaws of the lion and the bear. David's years keeping his flock safe from vicious predators and singing songs to God in the pasture weren't just a way to pass time. God was building his character for such a time as this. As he strengthened himself in the Lord, he certainly relived the moments when he charged toward the Philistine giant Goliath with nothing but a sling and a stone. David remembered watching the giant hit the ground with a loud thud, sending dust flying. He remembered wielding Goliath's own sword and then returning to his comrades with the giant warrior's head in his hand. If God delivered him before, He would surely do it again! As he fellowshipped with his God and repented, David's resolve returned. Psalm 56 is a psalm David wrote when he was in danger from the Philistines and possibly one of the psalms of praise David used to encourage himself after the tragedy at Ziklag. It's worth the read. Let the words of the psalm soak into your masculine soul.

> Be merciful to me, O God, for man would swallow me up; fighting all day he oppresses me. My enemies would hound me all day, for there are many who fight against me, O Most High.
>
> Whenever I am afraid, I will trust in You. In God (I will praise His word), in God I have put my trust; I will not fear. What can flesh do to me?
>
> All day they twist my words; all their thoughts are against me for evil. They gather together, they hide, they mark my steps, when they lie in wait for my life. Shall they escape by iniquity? In anger cast down the peoples, O God!
>
> You number my wanderings; put my tears into Your bottle; are they not in Your book? When I cry out to You, then my enemies will turn back; this I know, because God is for me. In God (I will praise His word), in the LORD (I will praise His word), in God I have put my trust; I will not be afraid. What can man do to me?
>
> Vows made to You are binding upon me, O God; I will render praises to You, for You have delivered my soul from

death. Have You not kept my feet from falling, that I may walk before God in the light of the living?[3]

David could strengthen himself in the Lord that way because he *knew* the Lord. He had a living relationship with Him. Though he was hardheaded at times, David was indeed a man after God's own heart. "When my father and my mother forsake me," wrote David, "then the LORD will take me up."[4] David's foundation, strength, and security were rooted in the Lord, not in his circumstances, in his failures or victories, or even in his relationships with others, including his parents. He could encourage himself in the Lord because the Lord was his source.

Men today need to know where to get strength and empowerment for forgiveness and cleansing. It's not online or at a ball game or even hanging with the guys. Sometimes you have to leave the crowd, get alone with God, and cry out to Him until you find Him—and don't let go until your empowerment and transformation come. There's power in crying out. "Call upon me in the day of trouble," declares the Lord. "I will deliver you, and you shall glorify me."[5] There's power in renewing your mind as well: "Do not be conformed to this world, but be transformed by the renewal of your mind, that by testing you may discern what is the will of God, what is good and acceptable and perfect."[6] Being *conformed* to this world doesn't take effort. It just happens naturally. Renewing our minds with God, on the other hand, takes intentionality. It takes effort. When we are dialed in to Him, something supernatural takes place. We become *transformed* and experience the peace of God. This is what happened to David. He got back to the fundamentals with his God, got back in sync. He got dialed in. As a result his whole countenance was transformed. Then David found out what God's perfect will was for the dilemma of Ziklag.

DISCUSSION QUESTIONS

Are you out of sync with God? Explain.

How do you go about getting dialed back in to God?

What habits do you practice to intentionally renew your mind on a regular basis?

SWORD OF THE WORD

David strengthened himself in the LORD his God.

—1 SAMUEL 30:6

PRAY ABOUT IT

Pray and ask the Lord to transform you by the renewing of your mind.

CHAPTER 15

Real Men Bring Comfort to Broken Situations

God's definition of success is really one of significance—the significant difference our lives can make in the lives of others. This significance doesn't show up in win-loss records, long résumés, or the trophies gathering dust on our mantels. It's found in the hearts and lives of those we've come across who are in some way better because of the way we lived.

—TONY DUNGY

WHEN THE ENEMY has stolen from you, you must rise up and take it back, just as David and his band of men took it back. They recovered everything. Yet part of taking it back is taking time to rebuild what has been broken down, both personally and relationally, and that requires taking action. Stephen Mansfield wrote, "Ultimately...you only know who a man is and what he believes by what he does. Not by what he sits around talking about. Not by what he says he feels. It's only when he acts—when he does something—that we start to know what he is. Action is character. Manhood is action."[1]

When it comes to the subject of rebuilding, we must be sure not to overlook Nehemiah. He is critical to our understanding of biblical manhood. A man who rose up in the face of opposition and dared to take action, Nehemiah took it back by leading the rebuilding of Jerusalem's broken-down and crumbling walls. God then used him as a mouthpiece to call the people of Israel to national repentance after disobeying God's laws yet again. He also brought great comfort. Did you know that the name Nehemiah in the Hebrew means "Jehovah comforts"?[2] By taking action to instigate the rebuilding of the wall and then making sure it got done, Nehemiah brought comfort to the people. Without walls the people were vulnerable and afraid. They lived in the constant fear of being attacked. The walls brought certainty and protection, security and comfort.

In addition to overseeing the building of the wall and leading the people in national repentance, Nehemiah cared for the least among the people. He cared for the oppressed, the helpless, the enslaved, and the poor.[3] He fed the hungry, redeemed slaves, and stood up for the weak. These are things a real man does.

A Little History Lesson

The time was around 445 BC, and Jerusalem had seen better times. Some five hundred years earlier Solomon had finally built the holy temple to David's and the Torah's specific guidelines. For several centuries, though there were enemies on every side, Jerusalem and the temple stood strong. Then in 587 BC a bloody siege by Babylonian King Nebuchadnezzar left the city and the temple reduced to rubble. Once again the Israelites were scattered and forced into captivity while God's beloved Jerusalem lay completely in ruins—the temple, the houses, the gates, and the walls.

About a generation later, however, the Babylonian Empire fell to Cyrus the Great, King of Persia, putting the exiled Jews under Persian rule. Just one year later Cyrus made an unprecedented move. Just as Isaiah had prophesied over a century earlier,[4] Cyrus suddenly released the Israelites, allowing them to return home from their exile in Babylon for the purpose of rebuilding God's temple.

Get this: Cyrus of Persia, a pagan king, announced, "The LORD, the God of heaven, has given me all the kingdoms of the earth and he has appointed me to build a temple for him at Jerusalem in Judah."[5] Who says God doesn't use pagans to promote His agenda? "The king's heart is in the hand of the LORD, like the rivers of water; He turns it wherever He wishes."[6] Cyrus made a pronouncement allowing any willing Israelites to return to their homeland and rebuild the temple. He urged their neighbors and those Jews who chose not to return to help finance the mission with gold, silver, livestock, and more.[7] This was unheard of.

Over forty thousand Israelites took the miraculous offer and headed home. Some, including the priests and Levites, settled in and around Jerusalem, while others returned to their original homes in Judah. This was a significant number, yet it was only a tiny remnant of the entire scattered Jewish population. Most of the Jews chose not to return but to remain in Babylon because they were established and living comfortably. The remnant that did return, however, rolled up their sleeves and took on the challenge of rebuilding the temple under Cyrus' authority. God always has a remnant willing to do whatever it takes. Still, rebuilding was no small feat, and because of constant opposition it took twenty-two years and two more kings! At last, when the temple was finished, a lavish celebration took place. There were feasts, dancing, and sacrifices. From that point on most of the Israelites still living in Babylon and Persia acknowledged Jerusalem as God's Holy City. They faithfully paid their annual taxes to the temple, and whenever possible, they made pilgrimages to Jerusalem to celebrate the holy days and feasts.

A Huge Oversight

So, does all this talk about a city and an ancient temple thousands of years ago relate to masculinity and men in the US taking it back? Yes, it relates significantly! The people rebuilt the temple, but they didn't rebuild the walls to protect what they had built. Think about that for a minute. It's commendable that the Israelites returned to Jerusalem and focused on rebuilding the temple. Clearly it was God's favor that allowed them to accomplish this great task. Maybe they assumed that with God making provision for them, they didn't need something as practical as a wall.

Big mistake.

Can you picture in your mind the massive and grand celebration going on for the rebuilt temple while the walls continued to crumble around them? It seems irrational and hard for us to imagine. Nevertheless it was true. While the temple had been built and looked great, the walls protecting the city and protecting the temple were broken down, and the eight crucial wooden gates remained burned.

The reasons for this huge oversight were numerous and convoluted, but mainly certain Jews and enemies of Israel didn't want the walls rebuilt. Because of their financial profit from Jerusalem, they wanted the walls to remain in a state of disrepair. The same is true in our nation today. Forces inside our country as well as outside our borders actually want our nation to fail. Often the two are colluding. It's a disturbing realization. It's amazing how enemies hate walls, both personal and social. It's because they want access to our goods.

As the years passed, kings came and went, but the enemies of the Israelites living in Judah and around Jerusalem continued to plunder and defile the city. By the time Nehemiah stepped onto the scene, Israel was facing extremely difficult times. The people were living in distress and reproach, and in addition to the walls, most of the homes inside the walls were rubble. Few actually lived inside the city. The answer to the problem was obvious, but once again, as unbelievable as it may seem, some of the Israelite leaders didn't want the walls rebuilt. They were corrupt, working in cahoots with Israel's enemies—the Ammonites and Moabites, two people groups that God had instructed His people to drive out of the Promised Land centuries earlier. But these enemies were back and even had territorial governors serving under the king of Persia. These wicked governors were constantly plying the king with their lies and distortions of the truth. Though they served the Persian king who favored Israel, they themselves hated God's people and desired to keep Jerusalem in ruins.

When we allow into our lives and families a culture's ungodly ideology and things that God has told us clearly to drive out, the accompanying consequences will pop up and bite us when we are least expecting it, often to our own peril. The broken-down walls of Jerusalem were a symbol of the failures, hurt, and disobedience of Israel. Yet Nehemiah showed up and led a revolution to rebuild from the ruins. We, like Nehemiah, can let God lead us to rebuild from the chaos and shame of our past and broken-down situations. The Holy Spirit will empower and comfort us as we bring comfort and protection to those entrusted to us. Rebuilding broken walls does that. The Holy Spirit sent Nehemiah to rebuild and bring comfort. "You sent your good Spirit to instruct them, and you did not stop giving them manna from heaven or water for their thirst."[8] Anchored by the Word of God, let the Holy Spirit send you.

DISCUSSION QUESTIONS

What rebuilding is needed for you to take back what the enemy has stolen?

Do not despair—God has a remnant willing to do what it takes. Are you in the remnant category? Explain.

Where is God leading you to rebuild from the chaos and shame of your past?

SWORD OF THE WORD

Comfort, comfort my people, says your God.

—ISAIAH 40:1

PRAY ABOUT IT

Pray for the Holy Spirit to instruct you on how to rebuild and bring comfort.

CHAPTER 16

Never Let Up the Fight

*If a man has not discovered something that
he will die for, he isn't fit to live.*

—MARTIN LUTHER KING JR.

"DO NOT BE afraid of them," shouted Nehemiah to the throng gathered in Jerusalem's central plaza, his voice fueled by faith, passion, and righteous conviction. "Remember the Lord, who is great and awesome, and fight for your brothers, your sons, your daughters, your wives, and your homes."[1]

When Nehemiah made this inspiring speech, he had already spurred a grassroots uprising. He announced what God had put in his heart to do and encouraged the people that it was not just his idea but God's. "So they said, 'Let us rise up and build.' Then they set their hands to this good work."[2] The people had responded enthusiastically to Nehemiah's call to action. But at the time of this speech, although work had begun and progress was being made, the wall was only half finished, and their enemies wouldn't let up. The constant bombardment was wearing the people down, making the task increasingly difficult. Demoralized, the workers wanted to quit. But Nehemiah was challenging them again, this time not only to keep building but also to fight—to fight for their families, themselves, their homes, their nation, and their heritage! When you try to rebuild your walls, the enemy will put up a fight. Building God's walls requires doing battle.

Nehemiah urged the people to remember who they were—God's chosen people—and that He was on their side. God would empower them to complete their assignment if they would trust Him to fight alongside them, to fight for them. They did not have to give in to fear. Neither do we: "For the weapons of our warfare are not carnal but mighty in God for pulling down strongholds."[3]

Weapons and Bricks

Women and children were in the crowd that day as Nehemiah stirred the people with his speech. Most everyone had pitched in to help work in some way, but mainly he was addressing the men. Without men the wall wouldn't get rebuilt. The fate of the city was in their hands. The ones that would do battle were the men. Nehemiah had military guards who had accompanied him on the thousand-mile journey from Persia, but most of the Israelite guys doing the labor weren't warriors. At least they didn't start out as such. They were regular joes—husbands, dads, single guys, farmers, blacksmiths, bakers, priests, you name it. But they were not just any old group of guys. They were God's chosen men who became mighty warriors, fighting a war while building a wall. "From that day on," Nehemiah wrote, "half of my men did the work, while the other half were equipped with spears, shields, bows and armor.... Those who carried materials did their work with one hand and held a weapon in the other, and each of the builders wore his sword at his side as he worked."[4]

Nehemiah and his team of wall builders had a task to do, a God assignment to accomplish, but at the same time they had to protect themselves from the enemies who were against them and their calling. It was work warfare, and it parallels every man's spiritual warfare. As you do the work of being the man God has called you to be, you need a sword at your side—and that sword is the Word of God. Paul's letter to the Ephesians says, "Be strong in the Lord and in the strength of his might. Put on the whole armor of God." It then says to take up "the sword of the Spirit, which is the word of God."[5] Hebrews 4:12 says, "For the word of God is alive and active. Sharper than any double-edged sword, it penetrates even to dividing soul and spirit, joints and marrow; it judges the thoughts and attitudes of the heart" (NIV). You must know how to wield the sword of the Word, and you must keep it at your side at all times as you build. Read it, memorize it, write it on your heart, so you are prepared for any attack the enemy might launch against you. The Sword of the Word sections at the end of each chapter in this book give you a good place to start.

To do anything in the kingdom of God, particularly to build walls of protection, a whole lot of wrestling, warring, and praying will be required, and the Word of God is your number one weapon. You can accomplish nothing without it. "For we do not wrestle against flesh and blood, but against principalities, against powers, against the rulers of the darkness of this age, against spiritual hosts of wickedness in the heavenly places."[6] The good news is that "no weapon formed against you shall prosper," and "if God is for us, who can be against us?"[7] For the walls of God to be strong in men's lives, it will require walking in faith, trusting God, and wielding the weapons of warfare against our spiritual enemies, while at the same time working on our wall with building blocks of character. "Life is a fight," wrote Florence Nightingale, "a hard wrestling, a struggle with the principle of evil, hand to hand, foot to foot.... Fight on, brave heart, courageously, the salvation of thy country hangeth on thy sword. Yield not an inch, let fall not thy arm, till the kingdom is fought for, the kingdom is won."[8]

Walls, remember, are important. They fortify and protect. They create freedom and comfort. The enemy hates them, but God wants men to build them strong. I'm not talking about walls that enslave or entrap, such as the Berlin Wall or prison walls or emotional walls and strongholds that keep us from moving deeper into God and relationships. Like the walls of Jericho, those things standing between us and what God has for us must be torn down so we can occupy our promised land. Then God wants us to build healthy walls of protection that safeguard our hearts and those we love. We're talking boundaries. "Above all else," the Scripture says, "guard your heart, for everything you do flows from it."[9] If you are a Christian man, the Holy Spirit resides inside you. Your heart is now the new temple for the Spirit of God to dwell in, and you must guard it with your life.[10] Nothing else is as critical—nothing. Everything you do as a man flows from within your heart—the way you love God, your wife, and your kids; how you conduct yourself on the job; how you influence those in your circle—everything. Guard your heart! Build a wall around it. The enemy wants to destroy it and bring you down. He uses past hurts, wrong beliefs about God's plan for you, wrong attitudes you've embraced through the years, and strongholds that prevent you from thinking clearly and seeing areas that God would have you fortify. The negative junk you allow inside your wall chips away at and weakens you and your relationships, starting with your relationship with God. A man can be building his temple, doing religious things, even spiritual things, that are all good, but if his personal walls are in disrepair, the enemy is going to exploit him. This is why you see men committed to church and involved in Christian programs who appear to be doing all the right things, but because of broken-down walls and temporary lapses, they are dominated by the flesh and its strongholds during the week.

Strong, healthy walls primarily do three things:

1. They keep enemies out.

2. They allow you to live in the relationship place God intended.

3. They give freedom to thrive to those within the walls.

Sometimes, as God's men, we have to fight while building our walls. We surely will have to fight to keep our walls strong. Our enemy's system of principalities and powers is relentless. They never stop. The war will rage our entire lives until we are face to face with Jesus. But we need not be discouraged or overwhelmed. We can have authentic joy, peace, contentment, and power. But it won't be our own power—it will be His power, the same power that raised Jesus from the dead, living in us![11] As godly men we can and must tap into that power.

What's interesting about the story of Nehemiah is not only did the men fight as they rebuilt, but they also had the priests consecrate sections of the wall and gates as they went along: "Then Eliashib the high priest rose up with his brothers the priests, and they built the Sheep Gate. They consecrated it and set its doors. They consecrated it as far as the Tower of the Hundred, as far as the Tower of Hananel."[12] They realized without God's presence and continual protection they would be sitting ducks. As we fight while building our own spiritual walls of protection, we must do it with total dependence upon God, consecrating everything with prayer as we move forward. Yes, warfare is a given, but it is also when we will see God's faithfulness and deliverance.

DISCUSSION QUESTIONS

Are you coming under attack as you rebuild your walls? How so?

Are you armed with your spiritual weapons? Explain.

How can you consecrate your walls as you rebuild?

SWORD OF THE WORD

> For the weapons of our warfare are not carnal but mighty in
> God for pulling down strongholds.
> —2 Corinthians 10:4, nkjv

PRAY ABOUT IT

Pray and ask God to strengthen your spiritual weapons for the battle. Ask the Holy Spirit to consecrate your walls as you rebuild.

CHAPTER 17

A Regular Joe

[God] uses burdened, broken-hearted, weeping men.
—DAVID WILKERSON

WHAT AMAZES ME about the story of Nehemiah, particularly the man himself, is it displays the incredible impact one ordinary man can have on his culture when he dares to believe God and take action. Reading through the Bible, Nehemiah just pops up out of nowhere. "Nehemiah who?" you might think as you scan the first verse of the Book of Nehemiah. It simply says, "The words of Nehemiah the son of Hacaliah." So who's Hacaliah? Exactly. Both father and son appear from virtual obscurity. In fact you will not even find Nehemiah's father's name anywhere else in the Bible. He wasn't from the Levitical tribe or particularly notable in wealth or strength. Royalty didn't flow through his family's blood. "Nehemiah the son of Hacaliah" is another way of saying Nehemiah was just a regular joe.

Yet because this regular joe, this ordinary citizen, had the guts to put feet to his faith, it triggered a chain reaction of men banding together with him. That seems to be a major theme throughout the Bible—one man stepping up to the plate, then a band of men rallying around him. Men rallied around Nehemiah much as they did David—except Nehemiah hadn't been anointed king. He hadn't slain any giants. Women and children weren't dancing in the street, singing his praises over battles won. Nope. Nehemiah had none of that. He was a guy with a secular job and a secular boss. He wasn't in the ministry. But Nehemiah loved God, was a faithful employee, and most definitely had some sanctified testosterone pumping through his veins. Maybe, in that sense, he was anything but ordinary. God delights in taking regular men with conviction and doing extraordinary things through them.

An Israelite by birth, Nehemiah had parents who had chosen to remain in Persia, which placed him there for the appointed time. Artaxerxes had become king, and eventually Nehemiah became his cupbearer. Though Nehemiah was an ordinary man, it doesn't mean he wasn't an important man. Nehemiah had influence. The final sentence of Nehemiah 1 says, "Now I was cupbearer to the king."[1] This was a pretty important job, but cupbearers were disposable and replaceable.

In those days there was no such thing as democratic elections. If you wanted to remove a king, you had to knock him off. One of the easiest ways to do it was poison. The cupbearer was the guy who tasted the drinks before they were served to the king. This position was an honor, and those chosen had stellar character and were considered very trustworthy. The king's life depended on it.[2] It's easy to see how a king and his cupbearer would develop a close relationship. The fact that King Artaxerxes chose Nehemiah to be his cupbearer tells us a lot. Nehemiah had likely begun as a common servant and worked his way up, gaining trust with each step. He did not become cupbearer overnight. It was an earned position of loyalty.

While Nehemiah was doing his thing in Persia, he assumed things were going along as they should in Jerusalem. Distance was a factor in those days. News traveled slowly, and the enemy leaders had deceived the kings in Persia into believing the walls were being rebuilt when they actually weren't.

One day Nehemiah got news from Jerusalem. "The survivors who are left from the captivity in the province are there in great distress and reproach. The wall of Jerusalem is also broken down, and its gates are burned with fire."[3]

More Weeping

The report grieved Nehemiah's heart. Just as David and his men did, Nehemiah wept over the sons and daughters and what was happing to his home city. He mourned and prayed and fasted. He cried out to God and confessed the sins of himself and of the children of Israel in not keeping God's commandments. He asked God to remember His promise that if they would return to Him, He would gather them back to Jerusalem. Nehemiah was convicted of the national sins of Israel, but he was also personally convicted to do the right thing, which meant taking action. He knew for God's people to prosper, the city had to be fortified with a wall. As he cried out and grieved, God put in his heart what to do at Jerusalem.[4] When an ordinary man grieves over how his culture has been reduced to rubble and how his own personal walls are broken down, and that man prays, don't be surprised what God puts in his heart to do.

The good news is this: broken-down walls can be restored!

Nehemiah started off as a regular joe, a cupbearer, but he became a warrior, a governor, and a spiritual leader of the people. What did God put in Nehemiah's heart to do? Go to Jerusalem and rebuild those walls. What has God put in your heart to do?

So, here's this regular joe, this ordinary guy with extraordinary character, and God put something irregular in his heart. It was big—way bigger than he was. Keep in mind too that Jerusalem was about a thousand miles away. This was before jets and fast cars. Camels can scoot but not that fast. Just the trip one way took three or four months! This was a big deal and a major commitment.

Although he had been a faithful cupbearer, Nehemiah didn't have the resources to pull something like that off. What Nehemiah did have, however, was faith, guts, practical insight, wisdom, a solid reputation, a couple of key relationships, and, most of all, favor—God's supernatural favor. One man with the favor of God on his life is a major force. And in Nehemiah's case, favor is what God used, and a whole nation benefited. Israel took back its prominence as a nation because one regular joe dared to believe God and step out in faith to make his God-given dream a reality.

And make no bones about it, Nehemiah was a masculine man. He was a builder. He wore a tool belt loaded with tools and a sword. He wasn't even thinking about gender but was fully immersed in his manhood, focused on the task God had put in his heart.

Divine Connections

Here's a nugget to latch on to: when God wants to use you on the next level, He quite often sends a person. The key to your destiny in God is often another person. There is power in one, but rarely does God use loners. He's all about connecting people. And don't try to limit whom God uses. God's provision doesn't always look like what you expect. The people God connects you with may look, talk, or act completely differently from what you expected or even prayed for. But don't miss out on the people God has sent to bless you just because it pushes you out of your comfort zone.

In Nehemiah's case God used a secular king, his boss. The king wasn't even an Israelite, but he was moved by Nehemiah's passion. When Nehemiah acted in faith and obedience, God responded. Just as God put it in Nehemiah's heart and King Cyrus' heart, He put it in King Artaxerxes' heart to help his friend and God's people.

Here's how it went down: King Artaxerxes noticed his chief employee was deeply troubled. For days Nehemiah had agonized about the state of the wall in Jerusalem. When the king asked him, "What's up? Why are you so downcast?" Nehemiah was moved to tell him the truth of what God had put in his heart. Now that was a risky move. The dude was afraid. I mean he was shaking in his boots. He knew Artaxerxes had the power to execute him then and there for even thinking about leaving. This wasn't the American governmental system with a ton of red tape and an HR department to go through before you get the axe. "God, are You sure about this?" Nehemiah must have been thinking. "You really want me to speak out and use my connections and position of influence with the king? He's not a Jew."

Sometimes God will put you in the right place at the right time to ask the impossible from the improbable. But it's going to take some backbone. When you recognize that's where you are, fortify yourself in the Lord, take courage, and speak with confidence. That's what Nehemiah did. He told the king not only why he was grieving but also what God put in his heart to do and then what it would take to make it a reality—time off from work, money, food, horses, guards, timber, tools, and letters of introduction.[5] Nehemiah asked the king to fund the project! Amazing! And Artaxerxes agreed! It was clearly a God thing. Remember, "the king's heart is in the hand of the LORD, like the rivers of water; He turns it wherever He wishes."[6] When God is on your side, He will even use secular people to help you. So, Nehemiah, the regular joe, gained momentum. He traveled to Jerusalem with the king's authority to check it out and then to get the job done.

The people caught Nehemiah's vision and rallied around him.

Their hearts were broken too. It was as if they had been waiting for someone like Nehemiah to rise up and take the lead. All eyes were on him and his all-out stellar work ethic, faith, and love for God. His attitude and faith were infectious. Nehemiah's dedication was a plumb line for those around him. Banded together, they got to work and overcame ridicule, distractions, skepticism, and physical resistance. In the end the wall was rebuilt in record time—fifty-two days! After its completion enemies and skeptics alike were amazed.

They concluded that only God could have done it. "And it happened, when all our enemies heard of it, and all the nations around us saw these things, that they were very disheartened in their own eyes; for they perceived that this work was done by our God."[7]

When men welcome how God designed them and they step up to fulfill their assignments without apology, God is glorified.

But that's not the whole story.

When word got out that the walls of Jerusalem had been rebuilt and there was now protection, Jews from all around began to flock back to their home, to the point that they had to cast lots to see who would live in Jerusalem and who would live in other cities. Nehemiah's obedience and risk taking sparked a national revival of sorts. After that he stayed in Jerusalem as a leader to serve the people and ensure the commandments of God were followed. It was a lifetime calling.

One man, one regular joe—whether he is a cupbearer or an accountant or a football coach or a teacher or a contractor—turned into a wall builder, turned into a spiritual leader can turn a life, a home, a kid, a church, and a nation around.

DISCUSSION QUESTIONS

Are you looking for the supernatural in the ordinary? Do you feel like a regular joe, like God can't possibly use you? Explain.

Are you faithful in the work you are doing? Describe a situation in which you were in the right place at the right time for God to use you.

God's favor opens doors and provides opportunities for you to do the thing He has designed you for. Are you tuned into possible opportunities? How will you react when God's plan isn't what you expected?

SWORD OF THE WORD

God has chosen the foolish things of the world to put to shame the wise, and God has chosen the weak things of the world to put to shame the things which are mighty.

—1 CORINTHIANS 1:27, NKJV

PRAY ABOUT IT

Pray for open eyes and an open heart to see the supernatural in the ordinary.

CHAPTER 18

Remnant Renegades

*When did we start believing that God wants to
send us to safe places to do easy things?*

—MARK BATTERSON

WHETHER A DAVID, a King Josiah, or a Nehemiah, regardless
of the period in history, God has always had His men who
were willing to stand up in the face of fierce opposition and do
what needed to be done. David's band of men who were taking it
back were no exception. We already know they were courageous,
tough, and battle tested. They were men's men, but they were so
much more. They were *remnants*, and they were *renegades*. The
two go hand in hand. They were remnants in that they were in
the minority. They were renegades in that they rose up in defiance.
Sick and tired of what had been going on in the culture around
them, they banded together to fight for what was true and honorable. They were men called to disrupt the flow of compromise.

It wasn't easy.

It wasn't safe.

Disrupting the flow of compromise never is.

Three unique qualities made these men *remnant renegades*:

1. They were frustrated with what they saw happening all around them.

2. They knew things could be better.

3. They put action to their faith.

It takes all three of these qualities before change can occur. It took remnant renegades to usher in the changes in Israel.

You remember the story. Saul was the reigning king of Israel. Before him Israel had been ruled by holy, God-fearing judges, yet the people weren't satisfied and wanted a king like other nations. God had anointed and appointed the prophet Samuel to lead them, but Israel rejected Samuel, which broke his heart. But God told him, "They have not rejected you, but they have rejected me from being king over them."[1] Think of it. God's chosen people, God's nation, no longer wanted God to lead them. Oh, they might have been religious, but their hearts were far from Him. Rejecting Samuel was rejecting God. Saul, on the other hand, had all the surefire signs of outward success. He was wealthy, charismatic, and physically imposing, and Israel demanded he be their king. So, God gave them what they wanted. Sometimes God will do that—give us what we demand, give a nation what they insist on.

Unfortunately Saul's kingship turned out to be devastating for the people of Israel. He was reckless and ruthless, in addition to being defiant of the Lord's directives. Finally God had enough and instructed Samuel to tell Saul, "You have done foolishly. You have not kept the commandment of the LORD your God, which He commanded you.... But now your kingdom shall not continue. The LORD has sought for Himself a man after His own heart, and the LORD has commanded him to be commander over His people, because you have not kept what the LORD commanded you."[2] God sent Samuel to anoint a shepherd boy whom no one suspected of being the next king. Unassuming in stature, David was the polar opposite of Saul. But his courage ran deep, and his heart was tender toward the things of God. When Samuel anointed him, the Holy Spirit came upon the boy and at that moment departed from Saul.[3]

From then on God's favor was on David. The anointing dripped off him and seemed to touch everything he did. Even Saul noticed the unusual peace that rested on David and recruited the lad to play music for him when he was depressed. David's music soothed Saul's soul. The king was so impressed with David that he made him his personal armor-bearer. Not long afterward, David slew the giant Goliath with a sling and a stone. David was on the rise. God showed him favor on the battlefield again and again; however, his time to lead as king had not yet come. Saul still held that position, and David was faithful to the reigning king. But Saul became insane with jealousy, and his love for David was replaced with a bitter passion to see him dead. Saul also began leading the country in a full-blown rebellion against God and His ways, making covenants with the enemy idol worshippers. The Torah was no longer being followed, and Saul's rule became tyrannical. God's chosen people, Israel, were living in a bondage of their own making—a destructive cycle of sin and oppression.

Convinced Saul was going to kill him, David was forced to flee and became a fugitive. Though he knew he was destined to become the king of Israel, David refused to retaliate and kill Saul. Instead he chose to trust, knowing that God would somehow, someway, place him on the throne, fulfilling His promise. But it had to be done God's way, in His timing. In the meantime David would be a remnant renegade for the Lord.

Then something amazing happened.

A remnant of men in Israel rose up and banded together with David. They knew God had anointed him to be king. They also knew David possessed a purity of heart toward the things of God and he longed to see God's ways restored to their homeland. They were renegades too and became fugitives with him. The Bible says, "All those who were in distress or in debt or discontented gathered around [David], and he became their commander. About four hundred men were with him."[4] Eventually that number would grow to six hundred. Most were ordinary guys. Many were considered outcasts, misfits, or leftovers. That's what the word *remnant* means. Referring to the people of God, the word means "those who are faithful to [God's] original truth despite apostasy and opposition."[5]

Contrary to some common notions, these guys were not lawless rebels with no respect for authority. They were honorable men. Some scholars contend they may have been "in distress over the state of their nation."[6] The phrase in Hebrew for *discontented* used in the scripture about David's men denotes they were angry, aggrieved in the mind, or discontented—probably with Saul's oppressive government. The phrase *in debt* in Hebrew refers to having "an exacting, cruel creditor...using their debtors with great severity." In Nehemiah 5:5, for example, such creditors were "taking away their lands and vineyards, and bringing into bondage their sons and daughters."[7] Many of these men rose up because they were tired of seeing their families and themselves in bondage. One pastor wrote:

> In David's time, if a man got in over his head, he could lose all he owned; there was no protection for those in debt. There should have been, and there was under the Mosaic law, but under Saul, the Mosaic law was ignored. These men came to David out of desperation because he, like them, had lost everything as he fled Saul.[8]

These men were beat up, discouraged, and displaced. So, they made a conscious decision not to take it anymore and banded together for change. God connected them in heart with David, and they became partners in purpose. They wanted freedom for themselves, for their loved ones, and for their nation. They wanted their culture back and for Israel to serve God again. No, these were not lawless rebels. They were remnant renegades who would eventually become known as warriors, men of valor—David's mighty men.

Remnant renegades who follow God become men of valor. Whether they are scaling the cliffs of Normandy to take back territory occupied by Hitler or taking back their families who have been occupied by the evil influences of this culture, men of valor fight the battles God has called them to. Today, because of lawlessness and apathy, the hearts of people in our society have grown cold toward right and wrong and the things of God. Common sense has gone out the window, as has morality. Just like under Saul's reign, when God's ways are tossed aside, tyranny becomes the rule of law and wickedness becomes the norm. Good is called evil and evil good—something that God hates.[9]

As a man, you may get tired of the fight. Your senses may get so overwhelmed and discouraged with the onslaught of evil and perverseness that you simply go numb. It's enough to make any man want to wave the white flag of surrender. You may want to check out and disengage from the fight.

But you can't.

You must not.

Too much is at stake.

Reserved for Him

Around 150 years after David and his mighty men had directed their society back to God, things had deteriorated again in Israel. The prophet Elijah became distraught over the defilement of his nation. The people had started worshipping the false god Baal, which meant uninhibited sexual immorality, alternative lifestyles, and child sacrifice. The wickedness had gotten out of hand, and Elijah fell into deep depression and despair. Convinced he was the only godly man left, Elijah cried out to the Lord, "The people of Israel have forsaken your covenant, thrown down your altars, and killed your prophets with the sword, and I, even I only, am left, and they seek my life, to take it away."[10] Many men feel this way, alone and isolated, as if the whole world is against them. Yet God's response to Elijah was, "I have reserved seven thousand in Israel, all whose knees have not bowed to Baal."[11]

God used those faithful men to preserve and take back the nation of Israel from destruction time and time again, even when they were in captivity by the enemy. There were always remnant renegades. There was Nehemiah, who was so grieved in his spirit about the condition of his homeland that he dared to man up and take a risk in the face of a culture riddled with enemies and unbelief. He was ridiculed by his own people, lied about, and hated by enemies. Yet God empowered Nehemiah with incredible favor, and he pulled off the seemingly impossible, saving Israel from certain ruin. Shadrach, Meshach, and Abednego refused to bow down to King Nebuchadnezzar's image, even to the point of being bound and thrown into a blazing furnace. God supernaturally preserved them, Nebuchadnezzar became a believer, and those three Jewish boys got promoted.[12] Daniel had an excellent spirit, and that excellence, which came from the Holy Spirit, elevated him and those around him. As a result Daniel influenced the whole nation and the king because he dared to take a stand for righteousness, even though he was tossed into the lion's den.[13]

Joseph—despite being hated by his brothers, sold into slavery, thought dead by his father, falsely accused of rape, and thrown into prison—manned up and remained faithful to what he knew God had promised him. As a result God's favor was on Joseph. He was promoted to second only to Pharaoh and used as a tool to save all of Egypt and his own people (Israel) from a devastating famine—all because he continued to trust God and His plan, despite his circumstances.

God even helped Joseph to forgive his brothers and bring healing to his family. Joseph had to choose whether to let his pain affect his actions in the situations he faced. Just as Joseph did, you have a choice. Are you going to live wallowing in your pain, or are you going to rise above it? When the famine was at its peak, Joseph's brothers traveled to Egypt to get grain and came face to face with their brother Joseph, whom they did not recognize. But Joseph knew. When he revealed himself to his brothers, Joseph wept so loudly that all of Pharaoh's household heard him.[14] People carry their pain. But Joseph took it back by not allowing his pain to dictate his actions and the course of his life. He knew living in bitterness is akin to drinking poison.

Remember, "your past isn't your past if it is still affecting your present."[15] Joseph rose above his past by showing grace. As the brothers were leaving to go back to their father, Joseph called out to them, "See that you do not become troubled along the way."[16] In other words, make sure you are careful so you get back here. Don't quarrel with each other. Joseph released them and released his pain. Joseph took back grace, forgiveness, and love. Joseph was able to see the bigger picture. He told his brothers, "But as for you, you meant evil against me; but God meant it for good, in order to bring it about as it is this day, to save many people alive."[17]

This is the stuff men have got to have in them to make it through this world. You may be in the midst of difficult circumstances. You may have been treated unfairly. You may feel alone or abandoned. But as a remnant renegade, you must choose to release the negative and take the positive. You must release the pain and take back grace, forgiveness, and love.

The list of remnant renegades goes on and on. The Bible is full of them—men such as Joshua, Caleb, Abraham, Moses, and Samson, just to name a few. All these men rose up and dared to risk it all by trusting God.

God uses remnant renegades to change nations…and locker rooms.

Two Locker-Room Remnant Renegades

In 1986 Florida State head football coach Bobby Bowden was faced with a choice: Would he rise up, or would he stay down?

In September, Florida State Seminoles offensive tackle Pablo Lopez was shot and killed after an argument. His death and the manner in which it occurred was a terrible blow to the FSU community and especially to the football program. Bobby Bowden called a team meeting the day after Lopez's death and had a frank discussion with his players about where Lopez was and where they would be when they died. He said, "Men, I don't preach to you guys very often, but I'm going to preach to you today.…I'm going to talk to you about something that doesn't have anything to do with football, and I want you to listen."[18]

Coach Bowden shared the gospel with his players as well as his own faith journey. He then said, "All you guys are 18 to 22 and think you are going to live forever, and Pablo thought the same thing." He pointed to an empty chair and said, "Where is he today? Where are you going to be?" He then told his players that his door was always open if any of them wanted to talk.

Recalling the incident, Bowden felt he had to speak truth to his players:

I feel I have a responsibility. These other professors can get you in their classroom, and they can talk about communism—that they are communists or atheists—and nobody bothers them. I feel like as a football coach I have a right to tell you what I think is right....I want you all to go to heaven; that's why I express this. It's your choice. I don't want to die without at least telling you what I know[19]

There were more people than just football players in the room that day. Assistant coach Mark Richt, who would later become the head coach at the University of Georgia, was also there. He recalled:

I stood in the back of the room as Coach Bowden addressed the team about what had happened with Pablo....He was talking to the players, and I just happened to be in the room, but he was speaking to me....I became very convinced at that moment that then was the time for me to live for Christ.[20]

Not too long after Lopez's death and the team meeting, Richt gave his life to the Lord in Bowden's office. Richt went on to have an impact for the kingdom himself. Coach Richt "is absolutely fearless in sharing the good news of Jesus Christ with others.

"Don't let yourself be silenced. Listen to that urging within you, telling you to speak up, to bear witness to the hope and faith within you."[21]

Remnant renegades, it is time to be bold. It is time to speak up and speak out. Don't let the world silence you. You are full of the Holy Spirit, and it is time to take it back and recover all! It is time to man up and fully embrace your God-given masculinity, offering that masculinity back to God for Him to use.

DISCUSSION QUESTIONS

Do you desire to have the spirit of a remnant renegade, willing to disrupt the flow of compromise in our society? Explain.

Do you have a spirit of courage and a heart toward the things of God? How so?

What are some circumstances in which evil was meant against you but God meant it for good?

SWORD OF THE WORD

So too at the present time there is a remnant, chosen by grace.
—Romans 11:5

PRAY ABOUT IT

Pray and ask the Holy Spirit to give you boldness to speak the truth in love.

CHAPTER 19

Talking Some Smack

God made me fast. And when I run, I feel His pleasure.
—ERIC LIDDELL, CHARIOTS OF FIRE

WE KNOW DAVID was a man after God's own heart. That's a big deal. But did you know that David was also a smack talker? The guy liked to talk it up. Sometimes rising up and taking it back involves talking a little smack. "Now just hold on a minute. That's pride, right? It's boasting. We are called to be humble. Talking smack is not loving or godly or humble. It's certainly not holy."

Oh really.

Actually, at the right time, under the right circumstances, talking smack is very loving, godly, even humble, and it can be quite holy. Eric Liddell, Olympic gold medalist and missionary to China, knew he was fast. He knew that when he ran, God's pleasure was pouring out on him. Confidence rises up in us when we are running in the lane God assigned to us, when we are doing what God made us for. This is true humility, and it is a key to biblical manhood. Self-abasement is not humility. Meekness does not mean weakness. Meekness is strength and confidence under control. It's a clear understanding of who God is—and that without Him we can do nothing, but with Him we can do whatever He has called us to do.

Our opponents don't stand a chance! David understood this, and yes, there is a time for some holy smack talking!

When David faced the enemy, in the form of the giant Goliath, he shouted:

> You come at me with sword and spear and battle-ax. I come at you in the name of GOD-of-the-Angel-Armies, the God of Israel's troops, whom you curse and mock. This very day GOD is handing you over to me. I'm about to kill you, cut off your head, and serve up your body and the bodies of your Philistine buddies to the crows and coyotes. The whole earth will know that there's an extraordinary God in Israel. And everyone gathered here will learn that GOD doesn't save by means of sword or spear. The battle belongs to GOD—he's handing you to us on a platter![1]

Now that's some serious talk!

Think of an All-Pro NFL linebacker chewing on a wide receiver, saying, "I dare you to try and catch that ball over me. You ain't nothin'! If you come across my turf, I'm gonna break you in half—lay you out, bro! Just try it." Or think of a championship boxer intimidating his opponent before stepping into the ring, as Muhammad Ali did to Sonny Liston. "After the fight I'm gonna build myself a pretty home and use him as a bearskin rug," Ali ragged on Liston. "Liston even smells like a bear. I'm gonna give him to the local zoo after I whup him."[2] Ali then proceeded to destroy Sonny "The Big Bear" Liston to become the youngest boxer ever to take the title from a reigning heavyweight champion.

Now, I'll be the first to admit that the type of smack talking those athletes do is mostly rooted in fleshly arrogance. That's trash talking, and it is distasteful. But I must admit that comments like Ali's sometimes make me smile. For good reason we want our heroes to have quiet confidence, to just play their games, and to shut the mouths of the trash talkers. We love it when they are forced to eat their words. Yet David's smack wasn't trash. It was birthed not out of pride or arrogance but out of righteous indignation. And with David, we're not talking touchdowns, championship belts, or gold medals. A nation, many lives, and God's honor were at stake. We all know the ancient story. Libraries of books have been written on it. Countless sermons have been preached about it. Flannel boards and Sunday school plays have depicted it—the epic showdown between a giant and a kid, a champion warrior versus a lowly shepherd boy. On one side about 150 pounds of armor and a spear, on the other side a handful of stones and a sling. When the dust settled, the giant was facedown in the dirt and the boy got the victory, the girl, and eventually the kingdom. It all happened because David was offended—he was offended for God. When he saw God being defiled and mocked, he took it personally. Holy anger boiled up inside him, just as it did for Jesus after He saw His Father's temple being defiled and turned into a den of thieves.

Jesus—a carpenter, a man's man with calloused hands and sun-baked skin—was outraged and started using a whip. Try to put yourself in that scene. If Jesus had a hammer in His hands, He probably would have thrown it or jacked it through a wall! The Bible tells it like this:

> When He had made a whip of cords, He drove them all out of the temple, with the sheep and the oxen, and poured out the changers' money and overturned the tables. And He said to those who sold doves, "Take these things away! Do not make My Father's house a house of merchandise!" Then His disciples remembered that it was written, "Zeal for Your house has eaten Me up."[3]

To drive them out, I'm pretty sure the whip sent a message. Jesus knocked their tables over, money spilling out everywhere. When you mess with people's money, they usually don't take kindly to it. But the dudes getting driven didn't want any part of Jesus. He was fully man, taking it right to them.

Jesus whipped His whip. David whipped his sling. When zeal for God and His ways consumes a man, he will use what's in his hand—maybe even a machine gun.

Holy Machine Gun?

The man trudging through the hot, dry, East-African terrain stopped to lift his sunglasses and wipe away the sweat stinging his eyes.[4] Standing there, he surveyed the parched landscape stretching before him then unscrewed the top on his canteen and took in a long, hard gulp. After securing the top back, he put the canteen away, adjusted his hat, and continued forward, moving cautiously. One always moved cautiously in Sudan. Even so, the man was ill prepared for what awaited him just beyond the next bush.

A ferocious lion poised to pounce? A crafty leopard? A black mamba, the most feared and dangerous snake in all of Africa, coiled to strike? Surely Sam Childers would have been equipped for any of the above. But he wasn't prepared for the sight of a young child—he couldn't even tell if the child was a boy or a girl—dead. The lower half of the child's body was completely gone, and what remained carried the decay, insects, and stench of death.[5]

One might assume the child had been devoured by a wild beast, but Sam knew better. He had seen this sight all too often during his short time in Sudan. The child was killed by beasts all right, the most dangerous beasts of all—terrorists. The young child had been blown to bits by a land mine. Terrorists had planted thousands of them around villages. One minute the child was playing soccer or chasing a pet or running an errand for his or her mother; the next there was an explosion that obliterated a precious life.

For several decades civil war has been raging in Sudan and South Sudan. Regardless of who's to blame, the Second Sudanese Civil War was one of the bloodiest conflicts ever, with one of the highest civilian death tolls of any war since World War II. About two million civilians died as a result of warfare, mass killings, famine, or disease because of the war, and four million more were displaced, many of them more than once.[6] Even though the Second Sudanese Civil War ended in 2005, the South Sudanese Civil War, the Lord's Resistance Army insurgency (don't be fooled by the name—they are not following the Lord), ethnic violence, and other conflicts continue in the present day. The terrorists will stop at nothing to gain control. They are ruthless. They are brutal. They are pure evil.

It's always the children, the women, and the families that pay the highest price in war. Often the terrorists raid the villages, killing the adult males before they set fire to the huts. They rape the women, then disfigure them by cutting off their lips, ears, and breasts with machetes. The kids are made to watch. Frequently they force the boys to kill their own parents and sisters. The terrorists take the boys and brainwash them. Over time, after witnessing so much killing, the boys become monsters themselves, repeating the same atrocities as their captors. It's hideous. It's repulsive. It's wicked. War is like that, especially when the battle is fought in your own backyard. Americans have a hard time comprehending it. September 11, 2001, gave us a taste—two airplanes used as missiles into the Twin Towers; people jumping out of windows, their bodies splattering on the concrete below; other people, including first responders, crushed under piles of broken debris.

Sons, daughters, mothers, fathers, husbands, wives.

You watched the television in disbelief. Then you cried. Why am I telling you this? Because war is horrid. It's cruel. There *is* an enemy out there who wants to kill us. You can cover your eyes and pretend it isn't real. You can try not to think about it. But it *is* real. Just ask the families of the victims.

An American, Sam Childers was in East Africa, volunteering his services as a construction worker when he walked up to the decaying half of a corpse that was once a living child. Sam knew he could not just cover his eyes. He had to do something about the atrocities he was seeing. But what can one man do?

A lot.

After sensing God's direction, Sam Childers literally picked up a machine gun and began to fight for the children, rescuing them. He risked his very life. Soon other men joined him in the fight, forming their own little army. Now the enemy fears them. Childers and his wife founded and operate Children's Village, an orphanage in South Sudan. In the past decade they've saved the lives of over one thousand children. Similar to a military compound, the orphanage keeps the enemy out, giving the kids a chance at life. The terrorists are consistently trying to kill Childers, yet time and time again God has supernaturally protected him. The enemy has also created various lies to try and discredit him, but Childers just keeps fighting for the kids. President Salva Kiir Mayardit of South Sudan said, "The Reverend Sam Childers has been a very close friend to the government of South Sudan for many years and is a trusted friend." President Yoweri Museveni of Uganda said, "Sam Childers is a long-time devoted friend to our government, and his courageous work is supported by us."[7] In 2013 Childers was the recipient of the Mother Teresa Memorial International Award for Social Justice. Other recipients of this award include the Dalai Lama. You can read more about Sam Childers in the book *Another Man's War*. Or check out his website, machinegunpreacher.org.

There's another amazing thing about Sam Childers. He'd be the first to tell you that he's a man with a checkered past and many flaws. Once a barroom brawler, drug addict, and sex addict, Childers was changed when Christ came into his life. However, it wasn't until he began to fight for something bigger than himself that he really began to live life to the fullest. A man willing to fight and even die in the process found real life.

What can one man do? A whole lot.

I imagine, like David, Sam Childers talked a little holy smack. When the zeal of God burns in your belly and that righteous indignation rises up, you might be surprised at what pops out of your mouth. I'm not talking about foul language. I'm talking the power of God's Word. When the Spirit of God jacks a man up, look out! God will use the gifts and tools He has placed in you to touch the culture around you and make a difference. When it's a God thing, when you're taking it back, smack talk equals faith talk backed up by action.

Here's the question: What are you willing to fight for? To die for? To live for?

There's another war raging, a civil war of sorts. It's been going on since the beginning of creation. Not to take away from the hideousness and pain of physical wars and terrorism, but this war is just as horrific and in some ways even worse. Jesus said, "Do not fear those who kill the body but cannot kill the soul. Rather fear him who can destroy both soul and body in hell."[8] Jesus also said, "For what will it profit a man if he gains the whole world, and loses his own soul?"[9]

There's a war of epic proportions going on for the souls of men, and it is threatening the very fabric of a generation. You can cover your eyes and pretend it's not happening, but it *is* affecting you and your family all the same. Land mines planted strategically by the enemy and RPGs flying around are knocking men out, destroying their souls, ruining their futures, wrecking their relationships, and taking them and their children captive. Are you ready to take it back?

DISCUSSION QUESTIONS

Have you experienced times when the Spirit of God rises up in you? Explain.

What does it mean to talk holy smack?

What are some ways you can fight for yourself and your family?

SWORD OF THE WORD

And they said, "Let us rise up and build." So they strengthened their hands for the good work.

—NEHEMIAH 2:18

PRAY ABOUT IT

Ask God to place His zeal in you to do His work. Ask Him to make you confident and courageous with boldness from Him, not from yourself.

CHAPTER 20

That Something

It won't always be easy.... Yet if you move in faith,
God will always breathe life on your journey. I
think that's the way the shepherd boy was thinking
when he walked into the Valley of Elah.

—LOUIE GIGLIO

Before he reigned as one of the most influential kings in the history of the world, David was alone and isolated out in the fields, tending sheep. His own father, Jesse, left him there when Samuel had him summon all his sons to be considered for leadership. It wasn't so much that Jesse forgot about David. Jesse just never even considered him a possibility. Why waste anyone's time with David? He was not important. Surely he wasn't qualified.

Talk about father wounds.

"Dark and handsome, with beautiful eyes,"[1] David was the quintessential kid next door. Unlike Saul there was nothing particularly warrior-like about his outward appearance. But David's personal security didn't come from his outward appearance or his earthly father. It came from his personal relationship with God. Inwardly David possessed something that set him apart and separated him from the average. That something would align the course for his life and elevate him to greatness. Until it was his time to shine, however, David had to remain hidden from the world in the pastures while God developed him in private.

When it was his time, though, that something rose up, giving David a supernatural confidence that sparked him. We're talking not about arrogance and confidence in his flesh but about courage beyond his circumstances, a faith in a God who he was certain had his back. David could do that because he knew his God. There is no natural explanation for David stepping up as he did, other than a relationship with a supernatural God who does supernatural things through ordinary vessels yielded to Him. That something was the Holy Spirit, who came upon David when Samuel poured the oil.

Just Another Mundane Day

It began pretty much like every other mundane day. David, who was between fifteen and nineteen years old, was given a simple assignment: to deliver lunch and supplies to his older brothers' camp, out by the battle. These brothers were part of Israel's army. Their job was to protect God's chosen people. They were also David's heroes. They were warriors whom he longed to be like one day. So, when he got the opportunity to go where the action was, he leaped at the chance. When David arrived, however, he found the opposite of what he expected happening, and he was appalled. Israel's great and mighty warriors, his brothers included, were all cowering while this enemy-giant Philistine and the other warriors taunted them. Goliath was mocking God and His people. Instead of manning up, Israel's warriors "fled from him and were dreadfully afraid."[2] While the Israelite soldiers retreated in fear, godly indignation rose up inside David. He couldn't take seeing his God and his people being defied. His assignment of bringing lunch no longer seemed important. He must have wondered, "How can you think about food at a time like this?" David, a man after God's heart, had a warrior's heart. While others just watched, David rose up and said, "No! Not on my watch. Ain't gonna happen. We're putting a stop to this nonsense right now!"

Historians tell us that possibly in an effort to minimize bloodshed, the Philistines had been issuing a challenge to the Israelite troops of one-on-one combat—the Philistines' best warrior, Goliath, against Israel's best warrior. It was winner-take-all and a common practice in ancient warfare. The challenge had been going on for forty days. The Philistines were relentlessly attacking God's people and imposing on their land. The problem was no one on Israel's side had stepped up, even after Saul's offer of a reward—great riches, his daughter, and a tax-free life.[3] You have to ask yourself, Why had no one stepped up? I mean, these were highly skilled Israelite warriors, some of the very ones who would eventually become part of David's mighty band of men. This giant Goliath, however, was one terrifying, imposing, fear-stirring opponent. He was a champion warrior with a battle history of winning, much like an undefeated heavyweight boxer with a string of knockouts on his record. Nobody wanted to fight the guy.

David saw what was going on and couldn't believe his eyes. He was outraged. That something inside him that set him apart—the power of the Holy Spirit—began to surface. David spoke to the men and said, "Who is this uncircumcised Philistine, that he should defy the armies of the living God?"[4] Not knowing it was the Holy Spirit, the men around David were taken aback by his perceived youthful arrogance. "He's just a foolish kid who doesn't know any better." Older, wiser men who are used to settling have a way of discouraging young men from stepping out and doing big things for God. Yet the Scriptures say, "Let no one despise your youth."[5] David didn't. When the Holy Spirit moved him to step up, others around discouraged him. This will happen to you too. When the Spirit empowers you to move, others will try to keep you down.

Then David's brother asked him, "Why did you come down here? And with whom have you left those few sheep in the wilderness? I know your pride and the insolence of your heart, for you have come down to see the battle."[6] When the Holy Spirit begins to emerge, those who don't have His presence and power will accuse you of being prideful, inexperienced, naive. But you must stand firm. David told Saul and the men, "Don't be afraid. Don't let your hearts fail. I'll go and fight this Philistine."[7] Nobody took him seriously—nobody except for God, that is.

When a man teams up with God, giants fall and walls get built. When the Spirit of the Lord comes upon you, things begin to happen. The Holy Spirit anoints men. Without His empowerment you can do nothing. With His empowerment David knew no bear, lion, or giant could stop him.

David knew things about himself and his God that the others didn't:

> But David said to Saul, "Your servant used to keep his father's sheep, and when a lion or a bear came and took a lamb out of the flock, I went out after it and struck it, and delivered the lamb from its mouth; and when it arose against me, I caught it by its beard, and struck and killed it. Your servant has killed both lion and bear; and this uncircumcised Philistine will be like one of them, seeing he has defied the armies of the living God." Moreover David said, "The Lord, who delivered me from the paw of the lion and from the paw of the bear, He will deliver me from the hand of this Philistine."
>
> And Saul said to David, "Go, and the Lord be with you!"[8]

Clearly Saul was convinced by the fierce conviction he saw in David.

The Separation Is the Preparation

While David tended his flocks in obscurity and the rest of the world seemed to be passing him by, a transformation was taking place deep inside his core. To rise up on the outside, you have to have something brewing on the inside. During all those years in the shadows, David developed a private relationship with and confidence in God. He didn't just know about Him—he knew Him personally. What did David do on those lonesome nights and days? Under the cool shade of a tree or perhaps a canopy of stars, he worshipped His Creator on stringed instrument and fellowshipped with Him. Worshipping in private is a serious exercise. What you do in private greatly impacts your performance in public. Nothing can take the place of alone time with God. The separation is the preparation. God prepared David for his moment. Empowered by the Creator whom he worshipped, David wrestled lions and bears while honing his skill with sling and stone.

The sling was a legit weapon and used in warfare. Hurling a stone with enough force and accuracy to kill took practice, a steady hand, and a keen eye. In modern times we tend to think of a slingshot as a toy or something you shoot for sport. But for David, out in the pasture, it was a matter of life or death for him and his flock. Slinging a stone with the skill David had was equivalent to firing a .44 caliber handgun.[9] This helps us see this situation in a whole different light. Yes, David was young, but he had a warrior's heart. And did you catch in the above scripture that he caught the lion by the beard and struck and killed it? He was not weak of heart. Handsome and boyish, yes, but make no mistake, David was also masculine.

David let God develop his character and skills during his time of separation. Then, when the right giant came along, he was ready. When David wielded that sling and stone, it was with the full power and authority of God's Spirit.

Holy Spirit White Moments

In sports psychology is a term called *white moments*. When athletes are having white moments, they are in what we commonly call the zone. Everything is clicking, and they can seemingly do no wrong. They mesmerize us with their performances, making the impossible look easy. Michael Jordan hits thirty shots out of thirty, gets sixty points, and sinks the game winner on the buzzer. Tom Brady, Drew Brees, or Ben Roethlisberger gets over forty completions and throws five touchdown passes against a formidable opponent. Those are white moments.

In sports, white moments are based on skill, talent, and preparation. A white moment occurs when skill, talent, and preparation meet opportunity. But there are other types of "higher" white moments—what we might call Holy Spirit white moments. That's when the Holy Spirit uses a man as a vessel to do something bigger and greater than himself. David had numerous Holy Spirit white moments when everything fell into alignment, God's favor was on him, and his assignment was the only thing in sight. No mocking or distraction could prevent him from achieving his goal. These moments were empowered and fueled by God.

Heisman Trophy–winning quarterback Tim Tebow had a Holy Spirit white moment in his now famous John 3:16 championship game as the quarterback for Florida. On that night, January 8, 2009, the BCS National Championship Game, he played an incredible game of football, but he also wore the scripture reference John 3:16 in his eye black. And during the game, that scripture was googled ninety-four million times. Millions of people read the gospel in a nutshell. It was bigger and greater than Tebow or a football game could ever be. And it made an impact on the culture. While Tebow was doing his thing and playing an outstanding game of football, God was orchestrating an all-time-high outpouring of His Word.

Tebow experienced a white moment during that impressive game. On the field he was a stellar leader and quarterback. The team was in sync. Tebow was dialed in, and the Holy Spirit used the young quarterback as a tool to touch millions of lives for Him.

When David killed Goliath, all eyes were on him, and he was dialed in. It turned out to be a defining moment that revealed God's favor was on him and God was there to back up the smack talk. It was David's Holy Spirit white moment.

Unconventional

When David stepped up and volunteered to face the giant, Saul tried to give him his armor. After trying it on and walking around a bit, David took it off. It was too clumsy, didn't fit properly, and weighed him down, hindering him from doing what he did best. Saul was a big guy, a head taller than everyone else in Israel. David was a teenager. Can you see how silly David probably looked? Well-meaning people will try to put stuff on you, weighing you down with good stuff that's not necessarily God stuff. David knew the difference. For a man to be effective against the giants in his life, he has to know the difference. But make no mistake about it—David didn't go into the battle unprotected and naive. He went fully armored with the stuff he had tested and trusted. He told Saul, "I cannot go with these, for I have not tested them."[10]

God wants you to go with your skills, gifts, experience, and talents. That's what God wants—what is unique in and through you. God made you a certain way for a reason. You need to be you. Don't try to be someone else. You cannot be successful in your God-given assignment while wearing or trying to wear someone else's stuff. When you rise up to face your giant, you must be exactly who God has called you to be and do exactly what God has called you to do.

> Then he took his staff in his hand and chose five smooth
> stones from the brook and put them in his shepherd's pouch.
> His sling was in his hand.[11]

Instead of doing things the typical way and going with the flow
of conventional wisdom, David chose the unconventional route. He
utilized and trusted the gifts God had placed within him, developed in him, and provided for him—faith, courage, character, a
sling, and some stones. David was walking in the power of the Holy
Spirit.

When David showed up as this unconventional kid with no
armor and no spear, Goliath didn't take him seriously. But it was
the edge David needed.

> And when the Philistine looked and saw David, he disdained
> him, for he was but a youth, ruddy and handsome in appear-
> ance. And the Philistine said to David, "Am I a dog, that you
> come to me with sticks?" And the Philistine cursed David by
> his gods. The Philistine said to David, "Come to me, and I
> will give your flesh to the birds of the air and to the beasts of
> the field."[12]

The enemy talks smack too! But the threats and intimidation
didn't faze David one little bit. Instead of cowering like the others,
David *ran* toward Goliath, full-out, with full confidence, slinging
that stone as he ran! Failure was never an option. Men who hold
back when God tells them to run full-out to the battle, who aren't
sure they are men, who are not certain God created them good,
don't get it done. Sometimes a man's got to get his crazy on!

In David's mind it was a done deal. The giant was going down.
And he did! A perfect shot, one smooth stone nailed the giant
between the eyes, sending him to the dirt with a loud thud. David
didn't have a sword of his own, so he took the giant's and cut off

his head. "When the Philistines saw that their champion was dead, they fled. And the men of Israel and Judah rose with a shout and pursued the Philistines.... And the people of Israel came back from chasing the Philistines, and they plundered their camp."[13]

There it is again—a man rising up, trusting God, refusing to sit back, taking a risk, and winning the battle and then others following suit. The actions of one man benefited an entire nation. Is there a nation waiting on you today? A relationship? A family? A classroom? A company? Don't let fear control you. Take action. Take it back by the power of that something inside you, the Holy Spirit. He will empower you to do what needs to be done.

DISCUSSION QUESTIONS

Have you experienced a supernatural confidence that you know had to come from something greater than yourself? Explain.

Have you experienced any Holy Spirit white moments? Explain.

Has God placed men in your life whom you can encourage and speak life into? What are some ways you can do that?

Armed with godly confidence in who God created you to be and what He created you to do, are you willing to run full-out to battle your giant? What giant are you facing today?

SWORD OF THE WORD

The Spirit of him who raised Jesus from the dead dwells in you.

—ROMANS 8:11

PRAY ABOUT IT

Pray for the Holy Spirit to rise up in you as you run to face your giants.

CHAPTER 21

Whom Are You Bringing Lunch To?

Your opponent may be larger in appearance, but if you have the Holy Spirit—God's deposit within you—the advantage is yours.

—STEVEN FURTICK

YOU NEVER KNOW when, where, why, or how, but be ready. What started out as a routine lunch errand for David turned into something way bigger.

It became a giant opportunity. Pun intended.

Though anointed to be the next king, David had remained in obscurity, faithfully tending sheep on the backside of a mountain somewhere. But everything was about to change. As David was handing out sandwiches and chips, Goliath stepped onto the scene and issued his challenge. And David stepped up. Little did David know, taking on Goliath would launch him into his destiny. Without the challenge of an enemy in the presence of his peers, David would have never been promoted to the next level. Hear me on this: God often uses an enemy to catapult you into your calling. But you gotta step up.

A man's giant might be his opportunity.

Don't despise mundane assignments. Facing giants is often preceded by routine tasks. If David had balked at the chore of taking lunch to his brothers, he would have missed his opportunity. If he had not been prepared mentally, physically, and spiritually to face a giant, he would have missed his opportunity. Be ready. Live ready. You never know when your giant is going to show up and issue a challenge.

From Water Boy to the NFL

In 1968, after earning All–Gulf States Conference honors as a running back at Louisiana Tech, Bob Brunet was drafted by the Washington Redskins. He played ten seasons, which included a Super Bowl appearance in 1973, and he was rated the NFL's number one special teams player during that time. In 2015 Bob was inducted into the Louisiana Tech Athletics Hall of Fame alongside such greats as quarterback Terry Bradshaw. During his induction, Bob Brunet was tagged as the "most improbable ever" to be inducted to the Hall of Fame.[1] What made his career so improbable? Bob got his opportunity while living in obscurity and faithfully delivering lunch to his brothers. When his giant showed up, Bob stepped up to the challenge.

You see, Bob Brunet encountered one unfortunate event after another that kept him from playing football until the playoffs of his high school senior year in the tiny, south Louisiana town of Larose. Go a few miles south and you fall into the Gulf of Mexico.

Brunet recalled, "They started a Pee Wee League when I was in the sixth grade. They had so many kids come out that they chose players for the teams by running a race. I was always fast and would have made the team but I had been very ill for a week and when I tried to run I couldn't do it—and I didn't make the team."[2]

Brunet couldn't play the next year because of his after-school job.

The next two years he was sidelined by injuries. As a sophomore in high school, he was not allowed to play because he had missed spring training due to his after-school job. Coach Lynn LeBlanc finally let him be on the team as a junior, but he didn't make the "traveling squad." Then Brunet was diagnosed with a slipped disc before football season began his senior year, but Coach LeBlanc let Brunet stay on as the equipment manager.

The team made it to the playoffs, but their top two running backs were injured in the last regular season game and couldn't play. By that time, Brunet had recovered from his injury, and the coach put him in the first playoff game as a last-ditch effort. Despite not having any previous playing time, Brunet played really well, and he was in the starting lineup all the way through the playoffs to the state championship game. Brunet had been faithful, and it put him in the right place at the right time to step into the opportunity offered to him.

During the championship game, a coach for Louisiana Tech was in the stands. He had come to watch some other players, but he liked what he saw in Brunet. After the game the Tech coach approached Coach LeBlanc and asked him about number 23. LeBlanc couldn't even recall that a number 23 was on the team. Then he responded, "Oh, that's my manager. We lost our starter to injury so Robert was filling in for us." That night, the Louisiana Tech coach offered Bob Brunet a scholarship, and he accepted (even though he had never heard of Louisiana Tech).[3] And the rest is history.

Brunet's opportunity showed up when two running backs went down and the opposing team was the threatening giant. He had to make a choice to lay down the water bucket and respond to the coach's call. I'm sure it was intimidating. After all, he had not been practicing or playing with the team. But he was ready because he knew what was inside him.

Here's a question for you: Whom are you bringing lunch to today? Your colleagues? Teammates? Coworkers? Extended family? Maybe your lunch is being faithful to your present assignment and paying attention to what's happening around you. What type of giant may be looming on the horizon? The people in your circle of influence may need someone to step up for them, a champion fighter to stand in the face of the enemy and declare, "The Lord God is with me, and He will prevail!" We need men to say they've had enough, men whom the world can look up to as examples of faith and encouragement, men who know what's inside them and are ready to do the right thing at the right time.

Maybe the giants you are dealing with are personal. They have been taunting you with fear, shame, rejection, failure, anger, addiction. These giants often have strongholds the enemy has fortified in you over the years. Giants can be people, mind games that derail you, things from your past that torment you, or negative thinking patterns, all of which seek to demoralize you as a man and keep you from following the path God has marked for you. But rise up. And look up. See the situation from God's perspective. Often before you can walk through the door of opportunity into a new season, you have to face the giant. "For a great and effective door has opened to me," wrote Paul, "and there are many adversaries."[4] Open doors are accompanied by adversaries. Just as David was launched by his giant, you can be launched into your destiny by your giant.

Let I Am Send You

Your righteous zeal must always be directed by God. You must know where your power comes from. David did. He shouted, "You come to me with a sword and with a spear and with a javelin, but I come to you in the name of the LORD of hosts, the God of the armies of

Israel, whom you have defied....The battle is the LORD's."[5] David knew if God didn't have his back, he was toast.

When Moses was a young man still in Pharaoh's house, he witnessed the horrible injustices against the Israelites. It angered him, and he rose up in the flesh, killing an Egyptian man. The consequences were that Moses became a fugitive on the backside of the desert for forty years. Yet God redeemed that time to get much of Moses out of Moses so He could actually use him. His time of separation was a time of preparation. Sound familiar? God is trying to do the same thing in you. To use men, God often has to allow them to be broken down so He can build them back up for His purposes. Finally, when Moses was broken down and weak, stuttering when he talked, God said, "OK, you're ready."

Moses said, "No way! I'm nothing. I can't even talk."

God said, "Good. Just tell them I Am sent you. That's all they need to know."[6]

Moses went forth with the power of God behind him. You can't do this mission without the power of God behind you. No way. But when you have the power of God, nothing can stand in your way! Regardless of their circumstances or conditions, I Am wants to send real men into every area of culture to make a difference for Him—coaches and cameramen, teachers and technicians, fathers and firemen, husbands and house builders. History is dotted with men who refused to settle and stepped up to defeat their giants. With I Am behind them, they changed the culture around them. They included men such as Martin Luther, the German monk who at risk of torture and death courageously nailed ninety-five theses to a church door in 1517. He stood up to the religious tyranny of the day and sparked the Protestant Reformation, which brought the glorious light of the gospel of grace to billions over the years. Four hundred fifty years later Martin Luther King Jr. was sitting at his kitchen table one night and heard the voice of Jesus say, "Martin Luther, stand up for righteousness, stand up for justice, stand up for truth. And lo I will be with you, even until the end of the world." Even though he faced giants "trying to conquer [his] soul," he listened to the voice of Jesus telling him "to fight on."[7] He listened. He obeyed. He stood up and led the civil rights movement, bringing honor and dignity to an entire race. Then there are guys such as Dietrich Bonhoeffer, Oskar Schindler, Billy Graham, William Wilberforce, and Johnny the FedEx man.

When you see Johnny driving up in his FedEx truck, you know something is different about him. He emits the peace of God. God often uses him to bring light and hope to those along his route. He sees himself as an ordinary joe who loves football, fishing, and hunting, just like most guys, yet he's a warrior, doing what has to be done. If you happen to run across him and his wife at the grocery store, you will quickly discover they are best friends, even after over thirty years of marriage. In church Johnny's wife and their grown son and daughter are often by his side. The family is a wonderful testimony to the power of God. They've gone on mission trips to Uganda, helped birth a church, and poured their lives into children's ministry. More than anything Johnny loves to worship God and pray. But it wasn't always that way. They've had their struggles and pain to overcome. Johnny had to make some choices. And at his giant moment he chose to man up.

Johnny will be the first to tell you that in his younger days he was arrogant, proud, and untamed. Johnny loved running with the guys and partying, despite his wife's pleadings to focus on their marriage. One night everything came to a head. His wife confronted him and gave him an ultimatum. Johnny can describe the next thing that happened only as supernatural. "We sat at the kitchen table, facing each other. No voices were raised. It was settled. I would leave. When I walked into the bedroom to pack, suddenly I had a vision. In my mind's eye I saw a high, steep, sloped road. Scattered all along the roadside was wreckage and at the end was a huge pile of wreckage. Then a voice spoke in my heart. 'This will be your life if you persist. You need Me.' I knew it was Jesus."

Surprisingly Johnny continued to rebel against God's call and stubbornly persisted in his path, leaving wreckage along the way. However, he couldn't outrun the relentless love pursuit of the Holy Spirit. Eventually Johnny hit a wall and had to make a choice. He manned up by bowing down to the Lord and then taking on his giants. Johnny started making a difference and is still making a difference today, one person at a time. Like the stats back in chapter 11 show—the powerful impact of a husband and father choosing God—Johnny's wife and children, the loves of his life, are impacted by his influence and making a difference in this dark culture.

When Johnny made a commitment to serve the Creator rather than the creation, most of his friends, like David's brothers, didn't encourage him. On the contrary, they tried to keep him down. "What? You're getting all religious on us now?" they mocked. "It'll never last. You'll be back. Just wait and see." Johnny didn't listen, though. He saved his soul and his marriage, and he began a legacy. Has it been a fight? You bet. Every step of the way has been contested by the enemy. But Johnny's fighting with I Am inside him, and it's been worth every second. In the meantime he keeps bringing lunch to people every day, taking on giants one at a time when they show up.

DISCUSSION QUESTIONS

Whom are you bringing lunch to today?

What opportunities have come into your life, and what giants did you face?

How can the giants you are facing raise others to a new level?

Are you in a position to hear from God, and are you ready to go when He says so? Explain.

SWORD OF THE WORD

The battle is the LORD's.

—1 SAMUEL 17:47

PRAY ABOUT IT

If you have been trying to fight your battles in your own strength, pray and ask the Lord to help you remember the battle—and the victory—belong to Him.

CHAPTER 22

Something Deeper Going On

The law of self-sacrificing love is
the supreme law of heaven.

—JAMES PAPPAS JR.

DAVID'S MOUTH WAS dry and parched from the journey. When he swallowed, his throat felt like balls of camel hair had been stuffed down in it, soaking up every last molecule of moisture. He was beyond thirsty.

Picking up his sheepskin water bag, he brought the spout to his cracked lips and sucked in a long, hard gulp. Grimacing, he jerked the bag away and stared at it for a moment, shaking his head in dissatisfaction. The liquid was borderline hot, lukewarm at best, accompanied by a foul odor like that of sealed-up floodwater. It wasn't of course. It was safe drinking water he had packed and carried for survival. "At least it's wet," he must have thought. What David really wanted was some fresh, cool, spring water—water that would revive his weary body and replenish his soul.

For a moment his mind drifted back to his encounter with Goliath. He had nailed the Philistine champion with a stone wielded by his trusted sling, but it was the Holy Spirit who directed its course, sending Goliath to the ground with a thud and putting the rest of those Philistines to flight. Yes, it was a great victory, but they were back. Like a swarm of pesky flies, the Philistines were always back. David now had three adversaries stalking him who wanted his band of men eradicated from the face of the earth—King Saul, the Amalekites, and the Philistines. Every move he and his men made had to be carefully calculated in consideration of their enemies who were always lurking about.

Sitting in the flickering shadows deep inside the cave's innermost chamber, David envisioned himself standing outside, high on the rocky ridge, taking in the fresh breeze and warm sunshine while gazing out over the breathtaking Valley of Rephaim. It was harvesttime, and the fields were a striking blend of brown, green, and gold. The aroma of frankincense oozing from the Boswellia trees hung heavy in the air. Weary of being on the run, David missed home. Though the cave of Adullam was more of a cavern, with tunnels and chambers big enough to comfortably house a thousand men, he'd been inside it for way too long. The claustrophobia was messing with his mind. He yearned to walk freely in the open air. Yet it was extremely dangerous outside at the moment. That was why he was hiding out in the wilderness cave with some of his men. God would let him know the right time to move. He had led him thus far. He would not fail him.

"Those wicked Philistines," he mumbled, pondering how they had captured Bethlehem, located just on the other side of the valley. Bethlehem was the town where he had grown up and played as a boy, the town outside of which he tended sheep, where God had delivered him and his flock from the mouths of lions and bears, where Samuel the prophet had drenched his head with oil, anointing him as the future king of Israel. David also knew that near the heavily guarded gates of his hometown was the freshwater wellspring where he had replenished himself so many times. Water, to ancient Middle Eastern people, was more valuable than gold. You couldn't drink gold. Gold wouldn't grow your crops, sustain your life, or refresh your weary body. Yes, water was a precious commodity, especially a sparkling well that sprung up from the crystal springs running below the hard, rocky soil. The Philistines' taking occupation of his hometown and its water source, making it their stronghold, was no accident. It was a strategic military move, and like a dull saw blade it gnawed away at David's guts. The thought of throwing the water bag against the cave's stone-cold wall shot across his mind. His hand gripped the sheepskin, but then he released it. He couldn't waste the water. He would need it.

Just then David's intense thoughts were shattered by the clatter of three of his thirty chief warriors approaching in the cave's corridor. They loved David passionately. All he had to do was give the order and any one of them would lay down his life for David. Of this he was certain.

After warmly greeting their warrior-king-to-be, the men attempted to discuss military matters, yet David struggled to listen, distracted by his inner seething mixed with an ever-growing urge to drink water from the wellspring at Bethlehem. The more he focused on the fact that the enemy was occupying the only home he had known, defiling it by their very presence, the more his resentment and thirst intensified. This craving for a taste of cool, crisp water from home was ruling him. Then, in a moment of weakness, David cried out, "Oh, that someone would give me water to drink from the well of Bethlehem that is by the gate!"[1]

The moment the impulsive words escaped his mouth, David wished he could snatch them back. But it was too late. They were released, bouncing off the cave's walls, exposing his heart and his secret longing. An awkward silence filled the hollow chamber. A fruit bat fluttered in the background. Looking at his three men with a pained expression, David let out a deep sigh and his shoulders slumped. A nod toward the chamber's opening was the signal he wanted to be left alone.

Pricked by the ache in their leader's voice and the longing in his eyes, the three glanced at each other, their eyes speaking what their hearts knew. These were seasoned fighters who had depended on one another for their lives countless times in battle. They had developed a bond closer than brothers. After fighting so many battles together, their thoughts were in sync. They were one. Love for and loyalty to their beloved leader rose up in them as flaming arrows. They departed the chamber—but only to do what they knew had to be done.

Later that night, under a canopy of brilliant stars, while David slept in the heavily guarded cave, the three warriors silently slipped away on horseback. If their leader wanted fresh water from the well at Bethlehem, then water he would have, even if it meant killing a hundred Philistines or a thousand—even if it meant sacrificing their own lives. Yes, they knew the risk was great. However, they also knew their skill sets. They were no fools. They were men, and they were warriors.

Love moves men to action.

After securing their horses at a safe distance, the three warriors wove stealthily on foot like foxes through a maze of boulders and bushes, ducking behind walls and fences, breaking past the enemy's outermost camp undetected and on to the wellspring. Located near the city gate, the well itself was not guarded because the whole city was under guard. Once several water bags were filled, the three men snuck back to their horses and galloped the fifteen miles back to the cave of Adullam, eager to present their gift.

When the warriors placed the water at David's feet and then bowed before him, he was stunned. Deeply moved, not knowing how to respond, the future king sat staring at the water. David's gaze shifted to his comrades. Fresh waves of gratefulness for his men's devotion washed over him, appreciation for their costly gift. Then, like a wielded stone striking him in the forehead, the full weight of the danger they had faced bore down on him.

David's throat tightened.

Tears formed.

His flesh longed to engulf the water, to indulge his thirst, to pour it down and over himself, refreshing his weary soul. It was an exceptional gift, an expensive one—one that represented love and loyalty, honor and bravery. Yes, he desperately wanted to drink, but something deep inside him, something stronger than his craving, rose up—the renegade spirit. David's heart ripped and he cried out, "Far be it from me, O LORD, that I should do this! Is this not the blood of the men who went in jeopardy of their lives?"[2] With that, David lifted up the water with both hands, holding it up toward heaven, uttered a prayer of thanksgiving, and poured the water out as an offering to the Lord.[3] Slowly the cool, crisp, precious water spilled out onto the floor, running down and around the men's feet.

Are you kidding me? Why would David do such a thing? What a waste! Surely God would have wanted him to drink the refreshing water. He needed it. He wanted it. Those three loyal warriors risked everything to retrieve it. The least David could do was graciously accept the gift, drink the water, and tell them how awesome they were—or if he wasn't going to drink it, maybe give it to them to drink! "Here, guys. You take it. I honor you for honoring me." But David's refusal to drink it and the fact he poured it out, even as an offering to God, seems, I must confess, a bit over the top and like a certain insult to the brave men. And surely it was—unless something deeper was going on.

Love Pours

There are myriad speculations and commentaries about why David poured out the water that day. No doubt, all sorts of emotions ran through his mind, including guilt and shame at his own selfishness for articulating his craving before his devoted followers, knowing full well the power of his words as the leader of such devout warriors. I believe, however, the ultimate, bottom-line reason David did what he did was because of the overwhelming love he felt for God and for his men in that moment and the love they had demonstrated for him. That which he craved so deeply was being freely offered. That is, it was free to David, but it could have cost his men everything. With this realization the water became less about a cool, refreshing drink and more about the representation of the sacrificial love his men felt toward him. They were willing to give their lifeblood for their beloved leader's desires. With that understanding, how could he drink?

Love moved him. Love broke him. Love will do that.

Whether it's risking all to serve someone you care about or saying no to something your flesh craves because you care about someone, love causes a real man to pour himself out.

It doesn't always make sense in the natural. The men's sneaking out to get the water didn't make sense. When David took on Goliath, the numbers didn't add up. Real men respond from their guts. That doesn't mean they are not wise and skillful, though! They don't do stupid things, but they respond with heart-driven action to what needs to be done. David's pouring out the water didn't make sense to the natural mind, but God's ways are higher than our ways. And God honored it, and David's men honored him. It was a gut-level love offering of gratefulness both to God for His faithfulness and to his men for theirs. It was an act of worship in response to the grace shown him, not something done as a requirement of the law, fulfilling some religious ritual. David could have drunk the water, but instead he took an opportunity to demonstrate his heart and the relationship he had with God and his men.

When as a man you live out of love as a response to the love and grace God has shown you, you begin to pour out to God and to those around you. Life ceases to be about you. Truly you begin to decrease as He increases in all the different areas of your life. This pouring out is not out of law or religious duty but in response to grace. It's not about doing more. It's about the condition of your heart, of your own brokenness and gratefulness. It's about grace and love for God and the ones placed in your life.

Sometimes You Have to Take the Bullet

Remember the seven mass shootings I mentioned that happened during the writing of this book? Amid the awfulness of each of those tragedies, someone rose up as a hero. One of them was a guy named Aaron Feis. He was the assistant football coach and counselor at Marjory Stoneman Douglas High School in Parkland, Florida. Feis sacrificed his own life while protecting his students. He was an ordinary man who poured out his life for the love of others.

According to witnesses, Feis sprinted on foot toward the shooter, shielding students from bullets, "and pushed at least one girl out of the line of fire" before he was shot.[4] Another article stated that Aaron Feis "died putting himself in harm's way to save others...running toward danger while others were correctly running away from danger."[5] Several kids are alive today and still have futures because Aaron Feis shielded them from bullets. Normally quiet and gentle, in a moment of crisis Feis took action as something rose up in him. What is it that causes a guy like that to rise up and take a bullet? Student after student testified how they knew that Mr. Aaron loved them. According to the *Miami Herald*, "On the last day of his life, Feis acted as a burly bodyguard to the kids he loved as his own."[6] Feis, in those precious seconds as the gunman wielded his AR-15, pushed aside his fear as love rose up, followed by courage. It was an automatic response prompted by love in his heart. There was no question of what the right thing to do was. For Feis it was instinctive.

Rising up and pouring out in moments of crisis is what real men do. It's what love does.

Sometimes it means pouring out the water, and sometimes it means taking a bullet.

But here's another question to ponder: Is it possible that there is something more important than taking a bullet? Now, I realize that is a difficult question. In that moment of crisis, when bullets were flying and innocent victims were dying, nothing was more important than the lives Feis saved, even though it cost him his own. The students alive today because of him would readily concur that Coach Feis' taking those bullets was the most important thing that ever happened to them. The parents and grandparents of those students would agree. Aaron Feis will forever be etched in our history books as a hero and rightly so. He gave the ultimate sacrifice, the ultimate act of love a person could give. Jesus said, "Greater love has no one than this, that someone lay down his life for his friends."[7] If you or I were called upon in that critical moment of crisis, I hope love and courage would rise up in us to take the bullet as well.

Yet there is something more.

Living Heroes

Maybe, just maybe, Aaron Feis would still be here today if a man had stepped up and been a living hero before the shooting even started. What is a living hero? When I think of living heroes, a few names pop into my mind. One is Joe Cullen. Joe and his wife,

Tahni, have one child, a fourteen-year-old, profoundly autistic son named Josiah. Nonverbal, Josiah is locked up in a world he can't escape. On hard days he's loud, acts out by hitting himself, and screeches. Josiah requires almost 24/7 care, and they can rarely go out in public as a family. It's a difficult life. Yet when you go to their home, it's filled with love and peace. God is there. It's obvious how much Joe and Tahni love their son. They are pouring out their lives for him. Joe has chosen not to live in bitterness or to check out. He shows up. He's fully present in Josiah's and Tahni's lives. Laying down his own life and dreams was hard. It was painful. It was not pretty. But Joe didn't bail. He's not absent. Instead Joe stepped up. As a result they are seeing incredible progress with their son. Because of his son, Joe has experienced a depth of character that few men reach. A godly, masculine man, he lives one day at a time, in the moment.

Another name that comes to mind as I ponder living heroes is a guy named Dale Kirkindoll. An ex-army sergeant, he is tough, intelligent, and definitely masculine; loves Jesus; and loves youth. He had to find a way to keep pouring his life into others, so he went right back to the frontlines of battle as a public high school teacher. Considering him a father figure, the kids love Mr. Dale, often confiding in him about life's troubling issues. Dale never backs down from telling them the truth, though. He shoots straight, and they listen because they know he loves them. Frequently at graduations his name is mentioned as someone who has deeply impacted them. Listen to what Dale said about real manhood: "To define yourself as a man the way the world defines masculinity—then it ends up in toxic behavior. But as a Christian, we should define ourselves as what Jesus says about us. The goal of every man's behavior should be to be like Jesus in the way he loves his wife, loves his children, does his work, and interacts with people. In order to do that, we need to know Jesus personally and have His Spirit in us. That to me is what real masculinity is."

Johnathan Fontenot stepped up to make a difference when he felt the call of God on his life to serve as a police officer. In a blog, he wrote, "Pursuing this job was an act of faith, in which I stepped out putting my trust wholly in God." He also wrote, "I am exposed to gross immorality, childlike behavior among adults, drunkards, fights, drugs, and many other things....I have to be strong and know that God will give me the strength I need to endure with patience all that I see. I have to constantly remember that I live in a fallen world ravaged by sin, but I also must remember that one day sin will be no more....It is no easy task, but I can do all things through Christ who strengthens me....I can emulate Christ by my character and treatment of others."[8] Officer Fontenot is definitely making a difference, being a light in a dark world. He's a living hero in my book. I salute him.

Living heroes are all around us—men pouring out their lives and taking a culture back!

Die Empty

Love for their wives and sons and daughters moved the men at Ziklag to pursue and recover all the enemy had stolen. Love for God and His name moved David to put his life on the line and run toward Goliath. Love for God and His people moved Nehemiah to rebuild the walls. Love for God and his men moved David to pour out the water.

If David had drunk the water, nobody would have thought any less of him, but we wouldn't be reading about it some three thousand years later. But you can equate reading about it in Scripture to God doing something special. It was a significant gesture that spoke volumes. Men who take the focus off themselves and choose to pour out their lives from love see God do special things, even supernatural things. And it's impossible to pour out in love if you are consuming.

In reality the only way to find true life is to pour out your life in honor of God and what He has done for you and in honor of those you love. Jesus said, "The man who wants to save his life will lose it; but the man who loses his life for my sake will find it."[9] Lose your life to save it? That doesn't make sense with the natural mind, but it's crystal clear. God's way to find your life is through losing it, by pouring it out.

Sometimes to take back his life and take back his culture, a man has to pour out the water. David wanted that cool, refreshing water. But when you love, you sometimes have to say no. You have to take a stand and pour out.

Now I realize a certain percentage of men out there are saying, "I've blown it. I drank the water! It's too late for me." Don't despair! It's possible to love God deeply and yet fail Him miserably. Don't let past failures define you. Let truth rise up in you and align your heart with God's heart, your spirit with His Spirit.

"For God so loved the world, that he gave his only Son."[10] Love moved the Father to action. Love moved Jesus to pour out His blood on the cross for your sins and mine. Love pours. Let your life be one of pouring out too. "Watch, stand fast in the faith, be brave, be strong. Let all that you do be done with love."[11]

DISCUSSION QUESTIONS

Is your heart in a condition of brokenness and gratefulness? Explain.

What are the areas in your life where God may be prompting you to pour yourself out?

What situations or areas does God want you to say no to so you can be in line with Him to hear when He tells you to move?

SWORD OF THE WORD

Watch, stand fast in the faith, be brave, be strong. Let all that you do be done with love.

—1 Corinthians 16:13–14, nkjv

PRAY ABOUT IT

Ask for the Holy Spirit's direction on when to move and when to stay put, when to say yes and when to say no. Thank the Lord for everything He has done for you.

CHAPTER 23

But What if I Drank the Water?

To see ourselves as we truly are, with all our
selfishness and carnality, would be devastating were it
not for the grace of God that shows us what we are
destined to be in Him—men of valor.... And
as we face the truth, He sets us free from the
past and from our deluded self to become
the men of valor He has called us to be.

—RICHARD EXLEY

I CAN FEEL THE despair rising up in countless men out there. They desperately want to take it back and be the men God created them to be, yet they feel as if they've blown it, that it's too late for them. "But I drank the water!" they cry. "I didn't do the right thing. I was selfish. I've hurt people I love. I keep failing again and again. It's no use. I'll never break free of this pattern of flesh and sin that I'm trapped in. There is no way God could love a man like me. At best, God's disappointed in me. I'm anything but a godly man. Why even try?"

My answer to each one of those cries is this: don't waste a moment's breath giving in to them. They are lies. Instead of despair, let hope rise up! I can say that because there is hope. No matter how deep of a black hole you've fallen into, no matter how hopeless your situation seems, no matter how badly you've messed up, no matter how many people you've hurt along the way, no matter how many times you've blown it—if you still have breath, there's room at the cross for you and territory to reclaim. In fact you may be at the greatest place in your life—the end of yourself. That's because when we reach the end, God's best begins. Only then can He truly get to work in us. Let's face it—if God gave up on men who failed miserably, the Bible would never have been written and His plan of redemption would never have come to be. The lineage of Jesus is a history of the broken, wounded, and seriously flawed. God delights in using cracked pots to fulfill His agenda and get His message across.

Consider these messed-up biblical heroes:

- Moses, the eventual spiritual leader of God's chosen people, started out as a hotheaded, anger-driven murderer turned fugitive. Moses was clearly playing the role of vigilante in defense of a Hebrew man who had been brutally beaten by an Egyptian. Even though he surely viewed his actions as justifiable, Moses let his flesh get the best of him and killed a man, then fled into the wilderness. Years later, after God had forgiven him, transformed him into a humble man[1] (forty years on the backside of the desert will do that to a guy), and used him to part the Red Sea along with myriad other miraculous things, Moses still struggled with an anger problem that cost him dearly. Because of his anger, he wasn't allowed to enter the Promised Land. Yet Moses appeared "in glory" on the Mount of Transfiguration with Elijah and Jesus.[2]

- Elijah, the prophet who called fire down from heaven, got so depressed that he just wanted to die.[3] He also appeared on the Mount of Transfiguration with

Moses and Jesus. Depression doesn't mean God has abandoned you.

- Jacob, one of the pillars of the faith, was a pathological deceiver and schemer. After Jacob wrestled with an angel, God redirected him and changed his name to Israel.

- Abraham, the father of our faith and called "the friend of God,"[4] lied out of fear and threw his wife under the bus to protect his own hide.

- Jonah, the pouting prophet, ran from his divine instruction to call a city to repentance, but God wouldn't let him get away. When Jonah finally and reluctantly obeyed, the city of Nineveh repented and God showed compassion on the 120,000 residents. Jonah wanted judgment and was so hacked off at God's compassion that he prayed to die. God rebuked Jonah for his callousness toward the lost but still dealt kindly with him, as with a son. Instead of punishing him the way he would have punished the Ninevites, God reasoned with Jonah to move him to repentance.

- Before Paul was an apostle, he was a terrorist who tortured, imprisoned, and killed Christians. Think of the pain he caused countless individuals and their families. Yet he became one of God's greatest spokespersons, and God revealed to him the New Covenant.

What about Peter, Samson, David, and many others? The list goes on. All these men carried serious baggage. Yet God not only restored them, but He also used them in incredible ways. God is in the restoration business, and He has not given up on you either. You can still embrace His life and live out a destiny re-created for you. The Holy Spirit will break the chains and demolish the strongholds that have you bound. He will heal the leanness in your soul and bring refreshment, joy, and peace. The Spirit will help you become the man you were created to be. When you know the One who is truth, you will be set free. The Holy Spirit is wooing, but the step of faith is up to you. Do you believe that God's grace is bigger than your past? "If you, O LORD, should mark iniquities," the psalmist penned, "O Lord, who could stand? But with you there is forgiveness, that you may be feared."[5]

Just Give Me One More Shot, Lord

Samson was anointed by God. He had it all—looks, strength, and brains. He loved creating riddles to stump his foes. He would give them a riddle to solve with a reward if they were successful. Samson snapped ropes when the enemy bound him, tore down massive city gates that weighed tons with his bare hands, and took on an army of Philistines with the jawbone of a donkey! Talk about a man's man. Samson may have made Arnold Schwarzenegger or The Rock look like a wimp. That's the way the Sunday school flannel-board figures depict him. It's quite possible, though, that Samson was rather average looking. That could be why the source of his strength baffled so many and the Philistines were forever trying to discover that source. If Samson looked like Hercules or the Incredible Hulk, people would have seen his muscles as the source of power. It's just a thought to consider. Either way works.

While Samson eventually revealed his hair as the secret of his strength, in actuality Samson's strength was the supernatural result of the Spirit of the Lord coming upon him. The Scripture is plain—it gives credit to God as the source of the mighty acts, not Samson's own might or his hair. In Judges 14:6, for example, it says, "The

Spirit of the LORD came powerfully upon him so that he tore the lion apart with his bare hands as he might have torn a young goat" (NIV). When Samson popped the ropes the Philistines bound him with and picked up the jawbone of the ass, the Scripture says, "The Spirit of the LORD rushed upon him."[6] Another passage says, "Then the Spirit of the LORD came upon him mightily, and he went down to Ashkelon and killed thirty of their men."[7]

The power was never in Samson's long hair. It represented part of his Nazirite vow and God's covenant to him. A member of the tribe of Dan, Samson was the last judge over Israel before the kings' period. Like David, he was also a warrior. His mother was barren, making Samson a miracle child from the Lord, handpicked from conception specifically to be a judge. An angel spoke to Samson's mother and said, "You shall conceive and bear a son. No razor shall come upon his head, for the child shall be a Nazirite to God from the womb, and he shall begin to save Israel from the hand of the Philistines."[8] Samson's hair symbolized the fulfillment of his side of the covenant.

Samson loved God, but he also loved women, especially forbidden women. As he became great in his own eyes, he began to pursue women outside God's plan for his life. Samson frequented prostitutes in wicked cities and eventually fell head over heels for Delilah from inside the enemy's camp. That would be like Captain Kirk from the *Enterprise* beaming himself over to a Klingon ship to have an affair while he had the secret code for the *Enterprise*'s protective shield! Delilah, the Philistine, led Samson on, but she had a completely different agenda than his. His was a fantasy love affair. Hers was to uncover the secret of his strength. Little did Samson know, his love toy was getting paid handsomely by the Philistine leaders to get this information. Day after day Delilah pressed him until, finally, in a moment of weakness "he told her all his heart." He let his walls down and let the secret slip out. "A razor has never come upon my head, for I have been a Nazirite to God from my mother's womb. If my head is shaved, then my strength will leave me, and I shall become weak and be like any other man."[9] Samson knew whom he belonged to.

Even though it seemed just the opposite at times, Samson did have a heart toward God and was a chosen vessel. But like a lot of Christian men, he foolishly dabbled in sin, playing with it. But any fool knows, if you play with fire long enough, eventually you will get burned. Proverbs couldn't be any plainer:

> …to keep you from the evil woman, from the flattering tongue of a seductress. Do not lust after her beauty in your heart, nor let her allure you with her eyelids. For by means of a harlot a man is reduced to a crust of bread; and an adulteress will prey upon his precious life. Can a man take fire to his bosom, and his clothes not be burned? Can one walk on hot coals, and his feet not be seared?[10]

Never forget this. Jot it down in your memory banks. There is surely pleasure in sin for a season. But you've heard it said, "Sin will take you farther than you intended to go, it will keep you longer than you wanted to stay, and it will cost you more than you wanted to pay." There was never a truer statement uttered. The writer of Proverbs put it this way: "'Stolen water is sweet, and bread eaten in secret is pleasant.' But he does not know that the dead are there, that her guests are in the depths of hell."[11] What began as sweet ends up bitter in hell.

This was especially true in the life of Samson. He was determined to push the envelope, the boundaries of God's stated will. Delilah had that look. You know what I'm talking about—seductive, dripping with sensuality, making promises she can never deliver but making you think drinking from her well will completely fulfill your wildest desires. Delilah was no fool. She cunningly made Samson feel good as a man, stroking his ego, and he couldn't get enough. She kept luring him until his walls were mush and he broke. With his guard down, she cast her bait, and Samson went for it hook, line, and sinker. The muscle man fell asleep in her lap, and the Philistines rushed in, clipped his locks, and bound him up. Note to men: never fall asleep in the enemy's lap. The enemy will often be in a seductive disguise. When Samson awoke, he figured he'd just snap the ropes and it would be business as usual. "But he did not know that the LORD had left him."[12] Samson was powerless, and the Philistines gouged his eyes out. He was blind without the Lord's strength. Many men haven't realized the power of God has left them, and they wonder why things aren't working for them. They are walking powerless.

The crazy thing is the whole time Samson thought that he was in control, that he could handle it. Isn't that what men think? They get proud and self-sufficient in their own power. They think they can handle it without depending on the Lord. Sound familiar? (David did it before the Ziklag disaster.) Samson ended up trapped, a victim of his own sin and foolishness. Nausea formed in the pit of his stomach because he knew better. Sometimes we are like the eagle that grabs the weasel and won't let go, and the weasel eats the eagle's heart out and brings it down. Sometimes we don't let go of stuff we need to let go of. "Why should you be intoxicated, my son, with a forbidden woman and embrace the bosom of an adulteress?"[13] It's insanity. It's all lies.

I helped a big-name guy who had spent millions on the most beautiful women money could buy. For years he had enjoyed their company as often as he wanted. According to the world and Satan's lies, this man had it all—every fantasy fulfilled. Yet he broke down and wept like a baby because none of it satisfied or brought pleasure anymore. All he longed for was a genuine relationship with someone who would love him for who he was and someone whom he could give himself to—one woman, one man, just as God intended. Men, don't be fooled and chase the fantasy. In the end it could cost you everything. It did Samson.

If Samson had only listened to God and obeyed. It wasn't that God wanted to restrict his fun or pleasure. God wasn't being a prude. He gave Samson boundaries and walls to protect him. But Samson went outside those boundaries, and the consequences were dire. His eyes were gouged out and his hair shaven. Then the enemy bound him in chains and threw him in prison, where he was forced to grind grain.

Sin will chain you up, and you'll end up in prison grinding grain. How many men have given their strongest and best years to the enemy and now they are blind and in chains? Is that you?

You may think God was done with Samson, and you may think God is done with you. But not so fast—grace is never done.

Samson's hair began to grow back. More importantly Samson's heart began to change. Pride was replaced with regret, shame, and godly sorrow. Once the leader of Israel and feared by the Philistines, Samson was led by a young man to a temple to be made sport of. Spectators were waiting on the roof of the temple, laughing and mocking. This was a celebration. They had been after Samson for years. He was responsible for a lot of destruction. While they were looking on in scorn, Samson told the young man to position him between two pillars holding up the structure. "O Lord GOD, please remember me," he cried out, "and please strengthen me only this once, O God, that I may be avenged on the Philistines for my two eyes."[14] In other words, "Just give me one more shot, Lord. Let me take it back one more time!"

In faith Samson chose to believe that God was with him again and began to push the pillars. It was his last opportunity for redemption. And guess what? God was with him! He was faithful to His covenant promise. "Then [Samson] bowed with all his strength, and the house fell upon the lords and upon all the people who were in it. So the dead whom he killed at his death were more than those whom he had killed during his life."[15] Although Samson had his weaknesses, he was a man of God and is included in the Hebrews 11 Hall of Faith.

As long as there is breath in you, as long as you call out to God, you can experience His grace, forgiveness, and strength. Certainly there were consequences to Samson's sin. There always are, but grace will always show up too. "But where sin abounded," wrote Paul, "grace abounded much more."[16]

Your Biggest Battle

One of the biggest battles you are going to fight as a man is during the moment after you sin. Sure, you left yourself open. The enemy moved in and rang your bell, knocked you back. You're staggering or even on the mat. Yes, you're guilty. You sinned with your eyes wide open. Satan knows this and follows up with punches of shame, unbelief, and accusations. The accusations about yourself are true but not the ones about God, like "God doesn't love you. He's so disappointed in you that you can't go back. He's angry and wants to zap you! Come on. Be reasonable. How could God ever love you?"

The enemy wants you to stay down. His greatest efforts are to get you to unbelief, doubting God. He doesn't want you to embrace God's promises and rise up. He wants to shame, silence, and sabotage you. The greatest victory Satan gains is when he gets a man to stay down because of unbelief and not get back up. It's a lot easier to just stay down. It takes resolve to get back up. David Wilkerson said it well:

> Guilt is dangerous in that it destroys faith. The enemy of our souls is not at all interested in making Christians into adulterers, addicts, or prostitutes. He is interested in one thing only, and that is turning Christians into unbelievers. He uses the lusts of the body to bind the mind.... Our real battle is not

really with sex, alcohol, drugs, or lust. It is with our faith. Do we believe God is a deliverer? Is He there to help in the hour of temptation? Are His promises true? Is there freedom from sin? Is God really answering prayer today? Will He bring us out of the battle, victorious? ...

Satan wants you to be so crushed with guilt that you let go of your faith. He wants you to doubt God's faithfulness.... The most important move you will ever make in your life is the move you make right after you fail God. Will you believe the accuser's lies and give up in despair, or will you allow yourself to receive the forgiving flow of God's love?[17]

When we choose to believe God, He responds by giving us a new assignment. Think of the apostle Peter. In the heat of the battle, in the pressure of the moment, he totally drank the water. Before him was an opportunity to pour out and support the Lord when He was taken captive, but instead of pouring himself out, he wimped out by denying Jesus not just once but three times. He even cursed about it: "Then he began to curse and swear, saying, 'I do not know the Man!'"[18]

Fast-forward to a few weeks later. Jesus had been crucified and resurrected. He showed up on the shores of Galilee after the disciples had gone fishing and caught nothing. Jesus shouted for them to cast their nets once more on the other side of the boat. After the nets filled to the point of bursting with fish, Peter knew it was the Lord, jumped out of the boat, and swam to shore. At that point Jesus asked Peter three times, "Simon, son of John, do you love me?" Peter was grieved because Jesus asked the question three times. He wanted Peter to get His point. Finally, Peter said, "Lord, you know everything; you know that I love you." Here's what you have to know: God knows everything. He was perfectly aware Peter loved Him. He was also perfectly aware Peter had failed Him miserably. Again, it is possible to love God deeply and fail Him greatly. But listen to Jesus' response: "Jesus said to him, 'Feed my sheep.'"[19] Grace forgives and always gives an assignment. From that point on Peter was a fisher of men.

Grace Pours Too

When talking about grace and forgiveness, we can't exclude David, who has been a central character throughout this book. David—a worshipper in spirit and truth; the man after God's own heart; the warrior who killed Goliath, ruled as God's king, and honorably poured out the water—was the one through whom the seed of Messiah would eventually come. The Book of Matthew begins by calling Jesus "the son of David."[20] What an honor for David. Yet, like all of us, David was a man of flesh and blood who committed some grave immoralities.

Not only that, David tried to cover his sins, which led only to more corruption. It always does. Just sweep it under the rug, don't deal with it, and act like it never happened. This is what he did for some time. I guess he thought he could hide it from God too. How many men do this? The only problem is, when the Holy Spirit is in you or on you, there is no hiding.

"For when I kept silent," David wrote, "my bones wasted away through my groaning all day long. For day and night your hand was heavy upon me; my strength was dried up as by the heat of summer."[21] Hidden sin will do that to a man. As long as David did not acknowledge his sin, it ate at him like an invasive cancer. There was no peace. Finally God sent the prophet Nathan, who pinpointed David's iniquity. We all know it. When David should have been in battle with his men, he stayed home. Gazing out the window, he saw a beautiful woman bathing and his flesh rose up. He watched. Instead of bringing his thoughts under submission, he let them grow to fantasies. Next he entertained the possibilities. Then David had to have her and turned his fantasy into reality. It's the usual path to sin. "But each one is tempted when he is drawn away by his own desires and enticed. Then, when desire has conceived, it gives birth to sin; and sin, when it is full-grown, brings forth death."[22]

The affair happened. Bathsheba got pregnant, so David ordered Bathsheba's husband, Uriah, who happened to be a faithful warrior-leader, to the front lines where he was sure to be killed. When it happened, David took Bathsheba as his wife, just as he planned. Back to business as usual. David had gotten away with murder, or so he thought.

One day the prophet Nathan showed up and read David's mail. God let David know he wasn't hiding anything. David was grieved deeply by his sin. At this point, David had a choice—repent and get right with God or continue in the path of rebellion. David was truly broken over his sin. Before, David poured out the water. This time he poured out his heart:

> Have mercy upon me, O God, according to Your lovingkindness; according to the multitude of Your tender mercies, blot out my transgressions. Wash me thoroughly from my iniquity, and cleanse me from my sin.
>
> For I acknowledge my transgressions, and my sin is always before me. Against You, You only, have I sinned, and done this evil in Your sight—that You may be found just when You speak, and blameless when You judge.
>
> Behold, I was brought forth in iniquity, and in sin my mother conceived me. Behold, You desire truth in the inward parts, and in the hidden part You will make me to know wisdom.
>
> Purge me with hyssop, and I shall be clean; wash me, and I shall be whiter than snow. Make me hear joy and gladness, that the bones You have broken may rejoice. Hide Your face from my sins, and blot out all my iniquities.
>
> Create in me a clean heart, O God, and renew a steadfast spirit within me. Do not cast me away from Your presence, and do not take Your Holy Spirit from me.[23]

God heard David's cry, forgave him, and then restored him. There were consequences, however. The son Bathsheba bore to David was struck ill by God. David did not eat for days and pleaded with God; he lay on the ground, prostrate, begging the Lord to spare his son. However, no heartfelt weeping could avert the child's death. When a man sins, it always affects more than just himself. Innocent people get hurt.

David dried his tears, "went into the house of the LORD," and worshipped God.[24] This is huge. David worshipped God. He wasn't bitter. He wasn't angry. But he was broken. David knew he would see his son again in eternity. He said it. "But now he is dead. Why should I fast? Can I bring him back again? I shall go to him, but he will not return to me."[25]

At this point David trusted God, put his past behind him, and moved forward in faith. Ed Cole said in his book *Maximized Manhood*, "If God forgives us, but we do not forgive ourselves, we make ourselves greater than Him. Wisely forgetting the past is part of man's maturing. It is essential to real manhood....Crying over spilled milk, living with regret, or carrying past mistakes are all wrong. Living with past mistakes is a mistake in itself."[26] David refused to be defined by his past sins and allowed God to define him as a man after His own heart.

Then something amazing happened. Grace happened.

David and Bathsheba had another son. His name was Solomon. And God allowed Solomon to succeed David as the next king of Israel. He endorsed Solomon and allowed him to build the temple David dreamed of. Solomon wasn't even David's oldest son, and there were other sons. On top of all that, Solomon became a direct ancestor of Jesus.

Now that's grace!

DISCUSSION QUESTIONS

Be honest. What are the deepest temptations you struggle with? How are you doing?

How have you drunk the water?

How can you personally relate to Samson?

Can you relate to David's failures and God's amazing forgiveness? Explain.

How did David move on?

SWORD OF THE WORD

Where sin abounded, grace abounded much more.
—ROMANS 5:20, NKJV

PRAY ABOUT IT

Spend some time in humble repentance before the Lord. Praise God for His abundant grace.

CHAPTER 24

Behold the Man!

Manhood and Christ-likeness are synonymous.
—EDWIN LOUIS COLE

Now, LET'S GET this straight—it's our opponents and the enemy who are creating all the confusion about masculinity these days, not God. He's not confused. God sent His Son into the world, with its systems and schemes and adversaries, as a man, not a gender-neutral effeminate. God knew exactly what Jesus was. "And being found in appearance as a man," says Philippians 2:8, "[Jesus] humbled Himself and became obedient to the point of death, even the death of the cross" (NKJV). As Jesus was ushered before the violent crowd, wearing a crown of thorns and purple robe, Pilate proclaimed, "Behold the man!"[1] Pilate didn't say, "Behold the person!" or "Behold them!" That doesn't even make sense, yet the term *they* has been designated as the new singular, politically correct, gender-neutral, nonbinary word now.[2] It's true. See the endnote. You can't make this stuff up.

Yes, Jesus was fully male and fully embraced His role. Not only was He the living, breathing Son of God; He was a carpenter/stonemason. That made Him a toolbelt-wearing, hammer-swinging, beam-lifting, rock-chiseling man's man who sweat beads and got calluses on His hands. The Greek word that is translated as "carpenter" in both Matthew 13:55 and Mark 6:3 is *tektōn*. This term could refer to a carpenter, mason, or metalworker.[3] Many scholars contend that Jesus was probably all three because most carpenters in the ancient Middle East had secondary skills in masonry and metal. I'm not saying you have to be a builder or work with your hands to be a man. You can be a man's man and teach kindergarten. My point is this: Jesus was a hardworking man. He wasn't a wimp. There wasn't a crisis of masculinity in His life. He didn't feel as if He needed to apologize for His gender. Jesus probably didn't even think about it, and He didn't identify as something other than who He was created to be. He simply lived out His days as a man, doing what men do. Again, this is not said to elevate masculinity or to put women in a lesser light. Men and women are equally important with unique roles that complement each other.

But Jesus was a man. Not only that, He was the perfect man.

All the great men of the Bible had elements of Jesus, but each missed the mark in one way or another. Jesus was fully man and fully God. As a man He was the perfect expression of masculinity in every aspect. So, if we want to know how to behave as God-created men, we must look to the One who was the perfect man. When Jesus loved, He loved perfectly. When He was angry, He was perfectly angry. When He spoke, He spoke perfectly. When He was silent, He was perfectly silent. He lived perfectly and died perfectly. Jesus wept and agonized in the Garden of Gethsemane, sweating drops of blood, a medical condition known as hematidrosis. He knew the pain and suffering that awaited Him, the floggings, the beatings, the nails, the cross. Yet courageously and humbly He obeyed the Father's call. This is love. This is masculinity.

Jesus showed compassion for the weak and challenged His followers. He healed all those who came to Him and caringly fed them. But the God-man didn't hesitate to call out untruths and hypocrisy.

He picked up a whip and loosed godly anger on those who defiled God's temple. He was not intimidated by the Pharisees who plotted against Him. He was real, hanging with sinners and rebuking the religious self-righteous. He spoke truth and let the chips fall where they may. Jesus drew lines in the sand and dared you to cross them. He was a strong leader for select men in His life. He poured into them, training by example. Jesus was direct and forceful when the situation called for it but also tender and patient. He wept over the loss of Lazarus. He demonstrated servant leadership when He washed the disciples' feet. Jesus is the living example of what a man should be—strong in the face of opposition, yet compassionate to those who followed Him. R. T. Kendall wrote, "Jesus is transparent integrity. Today we sometimes use the expression 'the real deal.' It is what people want to see in leaders, what people long for in relationships—no deceit, no infidelity, but honesty and trustworthiness. That is what we want in a friend—pure gold, the real thing."[4] I would add it's what both men and women want.

Though Jesus never carried a physical sword, He was the ultimate warrior. He was the living sword. "Calvary, the centerpiece of the Bible and that to which every biblical story and major character points, is the scene of the most outlandish combat in history," wrote Lieutenant General Jerry Boykin and Stu Weber. "The battle on that sacred high ground at Calvary was the D-Day of all time. Christ's victory on Calvary was declared not with a headline but with a resurrection!... Those who choose to characterize Jesus as a pacifist are entitled to that view, but I for one see Jesus as the ultimate warrior who makes clear that we must fight for justice."[5]

As men we are called to follow Jesus' example, to put on His character and champion those things that Jesus values. Real men champion causes, even the uprising of biblical masculinity. We can't ignore the attacks. We've got to fight and take it back.

Follow Me as I Follow Christ

The apostle Paul understood what we are talking about here. He was well aware that eyes were on him, watching every move he made. Paul was striving to be a godly example other men could emulate. In 1 Corinthians 4:16 he wrote, "Therefore I urge you, imitate me" (NKJV). He wrote again in 1 Corinthians 11:1, "Imitate me, just as I also imitate Christ" (NKJV). Paul wasn't being arrogant—far from it. He was ever aware of his old sin nature that kept rearing its ugly head and his constant need for grace in his life, but he also knew who he was and who was inside him. That's where his power was. "I have been crucified with Christ," wrote Paul. "It is no longer I who live, but Christ who lives in me."[6] Paul was aware of his weaknesses, but he was confident in his Savior, confident enough to tell people to imitate him.

As Christian men today we have to ask ourselves, Are we comfortable with our wives, our children, and the people in our circles of influence following us? Are we living the reality of Jesus' presence inside us so that it is transforming us into His image? This was Paul's desire: "...my little children, for whom I am again in the anguish of childbirth until Christ is formed in you!"[7] It bears repeating what Ed Cole wrote: "Manhood and Christ-likeness are synonymous."[8]

The call is going out not just for any men but for godly, Christlike men to rise up and take it back. Godly husbands, fathers, grandfathers, friends, and boyfriends who will step up to the plate. Single guys who will stand for purity and trust God for the godly women He has for them. Young men who will say no to porn and sex outside marriage, even if it means ridicule. Husbands who will love their wives like Christ loved His church. When godly men who know Jesus is real and alive rise up, God comes back, families come into alignment, and a culture is changed.

Why Women Should Love It

When a man imitates Jesus, he complements and supports women. He makes them better, stronger. Ephesians 5:25 exhorts husbands to "love [their] wives, as Christ loved the church and gave himself up for her."

How did Christ love the church? Well, for one, He died for the church. He obeyed God and suffered. Sometimes love suffers. Jesus washed His disciples' feet. Sometimes men need to wash their wives' feet.

Jesus elevated women in a society that didn't highly regard women. For example, Jewish men could mistreat and divorce their wives for the pettiest of reasons. Yet Jesus showed respect and honor for women, particularly His mother. His first miracle at Cana, turning water into wine, was at the request of His mother. Although Jesus said His time was not yet come, He did the thing she asked because it was important to her.

With the woman at the well, He publicly engaged in a theological conversation because she had a mind for biblical truths and questions. He met her where she was physically and mentally, and He gave her the answers that revealed Himself to her and freed her to receive ultimate truth.

Jesus taught a parable of a woman who had ten silver coins and lost one. He explained how she searched the house until she found it and called all her friends and neighbors over to celebrate. He likened this to the joy in heaven over one sinner who repents. What's not highlighted here is that Jesus chose to use a woman as the main character in this lesson when many would not place such value on this woman's cause. Jesus did.

He showed compassion to the woman caught in adultery, peering into her soul wounds and rescuing her from violent men, showing her what mercy and grace looked like. Jesus demonstrated how a man should treat women.

Jesus also had a heart for children. When the disciples wanted to send them away, Jesus told them to let the children come so He could bless them. Men with godly character take time for and are attuned with their children. They know how to play with them—from football and fishing to softball and dolls and everything in between—and intently train them in the ways of the Lord. This is pleasing to God. Spend time with your children and be fully present with them, not distracted or impatient. Let them see your example of love and respect for your wife and women so they will learn how to love that way too. Paul said, "But if anyone does not provide for his relatives, and especially for members of his household, he has denied the faith and is worse than an unbeliever."[9]

Jesus was about relationships with God and with people. He was all love and all man. When you have Christ in you, you can rise up and change the culture. The enemy knows if he takes down godly men, he can take down a family, a community, a city, even a nation. Arrogant, toxic men who don't respect women are pawns in the enemy's hands.

Jesus was the perfect blend of tenderness and warrior. He wielded a whip, but He also wept. He didn't stand for status quo or give in to the culture around Him. He took lashings. Make no bones about it—Jesus was a man's man. Ultimately it took a man to stretch out His hands and feet and take the nails. Jesus was the man, the warrior. Behold the man!

DISCUSSION QUESTIONS

What are some of the ways that Jesus was the ultimate man?

What are some characteristics of Jesus that go against the typical stereotypes of masculinity?

How did Jesus handle temptation?

How did Jesus view and treat women?

In what practical ways can a man love his wife as Christ loved the church? How can this be applied to single men?

SWORD OF THE WORD

> I have been crucified with Christ. It is no longer I who live, but Christ who lives in me.
> —GALATIANS 2:20

PRAY ABOUT IT

Ask the Lord to give you His eyes to see, His ears to hear, His hands to serve, and His heart to love.

CHAPTER 25

The Call of the Wild

Of all the paths you take in life, make
sure a few of them are dirt.
—JOHN MUIR

MY MIND YEARNED to disengage, to check out and lose myself in the wild. A group of four men, including me and my son, Zach, had taken a trip to the Alaskan Iliamna River area. Surrounded by rugged snowcapped peaks, the only way in or out was by boat or sandwiched into a small twin-engine plane. The latter had been our ticket. Only a few extreme mountain people populated the region. No stores. No medical facilities. No fast-food joints. No cell phone reception—nothing but raw, wild nature. You got the feeling you were all alone out there. Yet we quickly found out that this "raw nothing" was teeming with life. The brown bears and moose owned the land, while the salmon were just starting to run the river and the Arctic char were exploding out of the water. Our lungs sucked in the crisp, fresh air as the sound of water trickling from glacier-fed crystal streams soothed our souls. This was it. We were in our element as men, and it felt good. With the majestic mountains towering all around us, we fished together, laughed a lot, and got lost in the bush. Our time was rich with fireside chats, horseshoes, corn-hole, and, of course, fish stories. One morning when we woke to the brilliant sunlight, all I could think was "Wow!" The waters were pristine, and I could sense and feel the very presence and power of God like never before. It was a eureka moment. "This is it. God's here. And He's with you, and His heart is toward you." We got our gear and went fishing that morning. It was a time of bonding with one another like nothing else. When you're in the middle of nowhere with no electronic devices to pull at you, things get really basic. Time slows down, and the important things become very clear.

There's something about nature and a man. "Men cannot say they do not know about God. From the beginning of the world, men could see what God is like through the things He has made. This shows His power that lasts forever. It shows that He is God."[1]

Men are indeed without excuse. But it goes much deeper. God put eternity in a man's heart. Ecclesiastes 3:11 says, "He has made everything beautiful in its time. Also, he has put eternity into man's heart." We're longing for much more. We're longing for home. In the beginning God placed man in the most amazing, breathtaking plot of nature and fellowshipped with him there. Since the fall a drive or desire is wired in a man's heart to return to that place. He'll never be complete until he's home. The green trees provoke peace in us. The blue skies and purple majestic mountains take our breath away. Sitting in a cubicle or living in a cul-de-sac, our souls want to transcend the normalcy of life for the supernatural creation that awaits us. Women, too, hunger for and need this divine reunion with their Creator, but men often especially do. Part of a man's hunger is not only to be in nature but deep inside it is to connect with the God who created it and us.

The call of the wild is written in a man's DNA. It's how we're wired. When God created man, He placed him smack-dab in the middle of nature, and it's still buried deep within each one of us. Something's calling for us out there in the canyons to connect with our Creator, to live out our purpose, to know we matter—and to know God loves us.

What does all this have to do with the war on masculinity? Taking it back starts with getting beyond ourselves and daring to expose our inmost thoughts and desires to the Creator, who already knows them anyway. Somewhere in the depth of those mountains we met with Him, and He spoke—almost like Moses going to the top of the mountain. When Moses was done, he came off the mountain to do God's work. We can't always get to the mountains or the wilderness. We live in the here and now, in the real world of cell phones, traffic jams, deadlines, and, unfortunately, school shootings. Oh, it's a wilderness all right, and life has to go on. But we can, and must, still connect with the eternity that's in our hearts.

Charles E. Hummel's booklet *Tyranny of the Urgent*, published in 1967, soon became a classic. In it Hummel quoted a factory manager who said, "Your greatest danger is letting the urgent things crowd out the important."[2] Men tend to do that. In the urgency of the moment, the people God entrusted us with, the important things, and even God Himself—especially God—are put on the back burner. Hummel continued, "The root of all sin is self-sufficiency—independence from God. When we fail to wait prayerfully for God's guidance and strength we are saying, with our actions, if not our lips, that we do not need Him."[3]

When you slow down and connect with the eternity wooing your heart and submit your will to His, He places His desires in you. This is like coming down from the mountain. This is where fulfillment and purpose for something bigger than yourself arise. Otherwise you are wasting your dash—the time between your birth and death dates on your tombstone—or your mist. James wrote, "What is your life? For you are a mist that appears for a little time and then vanishes."[4] What's your epitaph going to say? "Hey boys, we took the hill. We got it done." Hanging on the wall in our home is a picture of the 2014 Liberty Christian Academy varsity baseball team from when they won the school's first-ever state baseball championship. It was signed by Zach's lifelong friend Josh—he and Zach played ball together from age five through college—with these simple words: "We did it baby!" They got it done.

And guess what? God is in the mountains, in the woods, on the crashing waves, and deep in the wild, untamed recesses of our hearts. God is not tame or safe, but we trust Him. The road that leads to nowhere is the road that leads home.

"Teach us to number our days," wrote Moses, "that we may gain a heart of wisdom."[5] That wisdom is understanding how God wants you to live and the assignment He has for you as a man. Here's the question: What are you going do with your mist, your dash? If you buy into the idea that God has something important for you to do, that He has called you to something greater than the urgent, then keep going because God's not done. Go get it done. The fight is still on until He calls you home. Press on, even though you are challenged on every side. Believe God loves you and is for you. Don't fall for the deceitful lies of the enemy. Fight the good fight. Finish the course. Keep the faith. Be strong. Embrace your masculinity. Act like a man. Be a man. Embrace the wild and the very essence or nature of God in all of it. Rise up and take it back.

The Bible says, "David, after he had served the purpose of God in his own generation, fell asleep."[6]

That's the ultimate epitaph: to serve the purpose of God for your life in your own generation, to make a difference for good in your own circle of influence, to love and be loved, and then to go home. Let this be true of all of us as Christlike men.

In one of my final conversations with my dad, he looked at me across a table at a barbecue restaurant and said, "Don't miss this,

Tim. If you serve Him with your whole heart, you will be blessed by Him. It's because of Him that I will see you again." It's just like David said to Solomon, "Show yourself a man." The baton has been passed. It's not too late. It's game time. Don't miss this. Go get it done. It's time to take it back.

DISCUSSION QUESTIONS

What do nature and creation mean to you personally?

Are you distracted by technology? If so, what are some practical ways to unplug so you can plug in?

Do you take time to slow down and connect with the eternity in your heart? What does that look like to you?

What would you like your epitaph to say?

After reading this book, what does *take it back* mean to you?

SWORD OF THE WORD

Teach us to number our days, that we may gain a heart of wisdom.

—PSALM 90:12, NKJV

PRAY ABOUT IT

James 1:5 says, "If any of you lacks wisdom, let him ask God, who gives generously to all without reproach, and it will be given him." Ask God for wisdom. Ask Him to help you fulfill the purpose He designed you for. Ask Him to make you a man after His own heart.

Endnotes

Epigraphs

1. Acts 13:22, NIV, emphasis added.

Introduction

1. 1 Kings 2:2.

Chapter 1

1. George Foreman with Ken Abraham, *God in My Corner: A Spiritual Memoir* (Nashville: Thomas Nelson, 2007), 195–197.
2. Foreman with Abraham, *God in My Corner*, 183.
3. Foreman with Abraham, *God in My Corner*, 184.
4. George Foreman with Max Davis, *Fatherhood by George: Hard-Won Advice on Being a Dad* (Nashville: Thomas Nelson, 2008), 24, https://books.google.com/books?id=328vd2WQMegC&vq.

Chapter 2

1. Ephesians 2:8–9.
2. Louie Giglio, *Goliath Must Fall: Winning the Battle Against Your Giants* (Nashville: Thomas Nelson, 2017), 121, https://books.google.com/books?id=Mmx7DQAAQBAJ&dq.
3. John Hawkins, "5 Reasons Masculinity Is Increasingly Coming Under Attack in America," PJ Media, January 20, 2019, https://pjmedia.com/lifestyle/5-reasons-masculinity-is-increasingly-coming-under-attack-in-america/.
4. Romans 3:10–12.

Chapter 3

1. Acts 13:22, NIV.
2. 1 Chronicles 22:8.
3. 2 Samuel 11:2–17.
4. Deuteronomy 17:17; 2 Samuel 3:2–5.
5. 2 Samuel 13:10–22, 28–32; 18:33.
6. 2 Samuel 24:10–15.
7. Jim George, *A Man After God's Own Heart: Updated and Expanded* (Eugene, OR: Harvest House Publishers, 2015), 14, https://books.google.com/books?id=_X5qBgAAQBAJ&pg.
8. Psalm 130:3–4.
9. Psalm 147:11, KJV.
10. Psalm 42:1–2, NASB.
11. 1 Kings 2:2, NKJV.
12. 2 Samuel 18:1–18.
13. 1 Kings 2:3, NKJV.
14. J. Oswald Sanders, *Spiritual Leadership* (Chicago: Moody Press, 1980), 24.
15. Matthew 5:6.

Chapter 4

1. 1 Samuel 30:1–4.
2. 1 Samuel 30:4, NIV.

3. 2 Samuel 23:8.
4. 2 Samuel 23:8–21.
5. 1 Chronicles 12:2.
6. Jared Mulvihill, "We Should Be Weeping," Desiring God, February 1, 2015, https://www.desiringgod.org/articles/we-should-be-weeping.
7. Charles G. Finney, *Principles of Discipleship* (Bloomington, MN: Bethany House, 1988), chapter 3, https://books.google.com/books?id=977kWtg2GLEC&pg.
8. James 4:8–9.
9. 1 Samuel 27:7.
10. Proverbs 25:28.
11. Luke 14:28.
12. Ecclesiastes 9:12; 1 Peter 5:8.
13. Ravi Zacharias (@RaviZacharias), "The biggest battle you will face in life is your daily appointment with God; keep it, or every other battle will become bigger," Twitter, April 21, 2014, 9:02 a.m., https://twitter.com/ravizacharias/status/4582745 14926063616?lang=en.

Chapter 5

1. 1 Samuel 30:8, NKJV.
2. 1 Samuel 30:8, NKJV.
3. 1 Samuel 30:9–20.
4. 1 Samuel 30:17–20, MSG.

Chapter 6

1. "Conservative Speaker Says 'Men Are Not Women,' Is Attacked, Sprayed With Chemical," New Boston Post, April 12, 2019, https://newbostonpost.com/around-the-web/conservative-speaker-says-men-are-not-women-is-attacked-sprayed-with-chemical/.
2. Jacey Fortin, "Traditional Masculinity Can Hurt Boys, Say New A.P.A. Guidelines," *New York Times*, January 10, 2019, https://www.nytimes.com/2019/01/10/science/apa-traditional-masculinity-harmful.html.
3. Noah Berlatsky, "This Father's Day, Men Are Experiencing a Crisis of Masculinity. The Solution? More Feminism," NBC News, June 17, 2018, https://www.nbcnews.com/think/opinion/father-s-day-men-are-experiencing-crisis-masculinity-solution-more-ncna884051.
4. "Toxic Masculinity in Boys Is Fueling an Epidemic of Loneliness," NBC News, January 18, 2018, https://www.nbcnews.com/think/video/toxic-masculinity-in-boys-is-fueling-an-epidemic-of-loneliness-1140033091929.
5. Goldie Peacock, "It's Time for Drag Kings to Detoxify Masculinity on TV," HuffPost, April 19, 2018, https://www.huffpost.com/entry/drag-kings-detoxify-masculinity_n_5ad8a00ce4b029ebe021a4c3.
6. Alanna Vagianos, "Terry Crews: 'Masculinity Can Be a Cult,'" HuffPost, April 16, 2018, https://www.huffpost.com/entry/terry-crews-masculinity-can-be-a-cult_n_5ad4cb42e4b0edca2cbc7b8e.
7. Guardian Staff, "Raise Boys as Feminists to Change 'Culture of Sexism,' Says Justin Trudeau," *The Guardian*, October 11, 2017, https://www.theguardian.com/world/2017/oct/11/justin-trudeau-pens-essay-on-raising-feminist-sons-all-of-us-benefit.

8. Neil Vigdor, "Patrick Day, Boxer, Dies After Suffering Brain Injury in the Ring," *New York Times*, updated October 18, 2019, https://www.nytimes.com/2019/10/16/sports/patrick-day-boxer-dead.html.

9. Gordon Dalbey, *Healing the Masculine Soul: God's Restoration of Men to Real Manhood* (Nashville: Thomas Nelson, 2003), 4, https://books.google.com/books?id=hbnPYQ_T-54C&q.

10. Stephanie Pappas, "APA Issues First-Ever Guidelines for Practice With Men and Boys," CE Corner, American Psychological Association, January 2019, https://www.apa.org/monitor/2019/01/ce-corner?utm_content=1546300435.

11. Noah Berlatsky, "Psychologists—and Gillette—Are Right About 'Traditional Masculinity,'" CNN, updated January 15, 2019, https://www.cnn.com/2019/01/15/opinions/traditional-masculinity-apa-berlatsky/index.html.

12. Leanne Payne, *Crisis in Masculinity* (Grand Rapids, MI: Hamewith Books, 1995), 82–83, https://www.amazon.com/Crisis-Masculinity-Leanne-Payne/dp/080105320X.

13. Brynn Tannehill, "10 Ways Right-Wing Christians Are Destroying Christianity," HuffPost, updated December 6, 2017, https://www.huffingtonpost.com/brynn-tannehill/10-ways-christians-are-destroying-christianity_b_8213708.html.

14. Thomas Gallatin, "Left media's Deliberate Mischaracterization of Christianity," Patriot Post, April 2, 2018, https://patriotpost.us/articles/55089-leftmedias-deliberate-mischaracterization-of-christianity.

Chapter 7

1. 1 Samuel 30:6, NIV.
2. *Southpaw*, directed by Antoine Fuqua, Wanda Pictures et al., 2015.
3. Ephesians 4:31.
4. Hebrews 12:15, CSB.

Chapter 8

1. Judges 21:25.

2. Romans 1:24–25.

3. Calvin Freiburger, "WATCH: Drag Queen Teaches Kids to 'Twerk' at Library Story Hour," LifeSite News, August 7, 2019, https://www.lifesitenews.com/news/drag-queen-teaches-kids-to-twerk-at-library-story-hour.

4. Calvin Freiburger, "Colorado Shooting Suspects Are Gender-Confused Girl and Boy Who Hated Christians, Trump," LifeSite News, May 9, 2019, https://www.lifesitenews.com/news/colorado-shooting-suspects-are-gender-confused-girl-and-boy-who-hated-christians-trump.

5. Caleb Parke, "College Student Kicked Out of Class for Telling Professor There Are Only Two Genders," FOX News, March 12, 2018, https://www.foxnews.com/us/college-student-kicked-out-of-class-for-telling-professor-there-are-only-two-genders.

6. Andrea Morris, "Keep Your Beliefs at Home: Student Booted From Class for Saying There Are 2 Genders," CBN News, June 17, 2019, https://www1.cbn.com/cbnnews/us/2019/june/keep-your-beliefs-at-home-student-booted-from-class-for-saying-there-are-2-genders.

7. Catharine Tunney and Peter Zimonjic, "Service Canada's Gender Neutral Directive Is 'Confusing' and 'Will Be Corrected' Says Minister," CBC News, updated March 22, 2018, https://www.cbc.ca/news/politics/service-canada-gender-neutral-1.4585629.

8. Brad Salzberg, "Justin Trudeau Bans Use of 'Mother' and 'Father' Within Government Organizations," Cultural Action Party of Canada, May 8, 2019, https://capforcanada.com/justin-trudeau-bans-use-of-mother-and-father-within-govt-organizations/.

9. Garrison Keillor, *The Book of Guys* (New York: Penguin Books, 1993), back cover, https://www.amazon.com/Book-Guys-Garrison-Keillor/dp/0140233725.

10. Michael Foust, "Court Bars Father From Teaching 6-Year-Old Son That He Is a Boy," Christian Headlines, November 28, 2018, https://www.christianheadlines.com/contributors/michael-foust/court-bars-father-from-teaching-6-year-old-son-that-he-is-a-boy.html.

11. Tasneem Nashrulla, "Two Parents' Legal Battle Over Whether Their 7-Year-Old Is Transgender Has Drawn a Child Services Review," BuzzFeed News, updated October 24, 2019, https://www.buzzfeednews.com/article/tasneemnashrulla/texas-transgender-child-custody-dispute.

Chapter 9

1. Matthew 4:11, NKJV.

2. C. S. Lewis, *The Screwtape Letters* (New York: Macmillan, 1943), 9, https://books.google.com/books?id=9zoPAQAAIAAJ.

3. Charles Haddon Spurgeon, *Spiritual Warfare in a Believer's Life*, ed. Robert Hall (Lynnwood, WA: Emerald Books, 1993), 78, https://books.google.com/books?id=x85si7tzDmQC.

4. 2 Corinthians 2:11, NIV.

5. Ephesians 6:12, NKJV.

6. C. S. Lewis, *Mere Christianity* (New York: HarperCollins, 1980), 142, https://www.amazon.com/Mere-Christianity-C-S-Lewis/dp/0060652926.

7. *Gladiator*, directed by Ridley Scott, Scott Free Productions and Red Wagon Entertainment, 2000.

8. Richard J. Foster, *Celebration of Discipline: The Path to Spiritual Growth* (New York: HarperCollins, 1998), 175, https://books.google.com/books?id=_92CMWUPv3UC&q.

Chapter 10

1. Jedidajah Otte, "Mars Colonisation Possible Through Sperm Bank in Space, Study Suggests," *The Guardian*, June 23, 2019, https://www.theguardian.com/science/2019/jun/23/all-female-mars-colony-possible-using-frozen-sperm-says-study.

2. Genesis 1:27, NIV.

3. Genesis 1:31, NKJV.

4. Nick Givas, "California State Senate Committee Bans Saying 'He' and 'She,'" The Daily Signal, January 23, 2019, https://www.dailysignal.com/2019/01/23/california-state-senate-committee-bans-saying-he-and-she/.

5. Billy Sunday, "Shew Thyself a Man," accessed January 24, 2020, https://www.biblebelievers.com/billy_sunday/sun15.html.

Chapter 11

1. Bob Horner, Ron Ralston, and David Sunde, *The Promise Keeper at Work* (Nashville: Word Publishing, 1999), 111.

2. European Population Committee, "The Demographic Characteristics of National Minorities in Certain European States: The Demographic Characteristics of

Linguistic and Religious Groups in Switzerland," CM(99)138 Addendum 5, October 27, 1999, table 9, https://rm.coe.int/16804fb7b1.

3. Horner, Ralston, and Sunde, *The Promise Keeper at Work*, 111.

4. Vern Bengtson, with Norella M. Putney and Susan Harris, *Families and Faith: How Religion Is Passed Down Across Generations* (Oxford, UK: Oxford University Press, 2013), 74, https://www.amazon.com/Families-Faith-Religion-Passed-Generations/dp/0190675152.

5. Roderick Hairston, *Cover Her: How to Create a Safe Place for the Ladies in Your Life…Physically, Financially, Emotionally and Spiritually* (Glyndon, MD: Strong Family Press, 2013), 12–13, https://www.amazon.com/Cover-Her-Roderick-Hairston/dp/1940786002.

6. "Research and Statistics," Rochester Area Fatherhood Network, accessed January 24, 2020, http://www.rochesterareafatherhoodnetwork.org/statistics.

7. Christine Winquist Nord and Jerry West, "National Household Education Survey: Fathers' and Mothers' Involvement in Their Children's Schools by Family Type and Resident Status," National Center for Education Statistics, May 2001, 31, https://nces.ed.gov/pubs2001/2001032.pdf.

8. James R. Dudley and Glenn Stone, *Fathering at Risk: Helping Nonresidential Fathers* (New York: Springer Publishing, 2001), 70, https://books.google.com/books?id=b5HSCgAAQBAJ&pg.

9. Meg Meeker, *Strong Fathers, Strong Daughters: 10 Secrets Every Father Should Know* (New York: Ballantine Books, 2007), 24, https://books.google.com/books?id=U06fudQ8CrAC&q.

10. "What Can the Federal Government Do to Decrease Crime and Revitalize Communities?," US Department of Justice, January 5–7, 1998, https://www.ncjrs.gov/pdffiles/172210.pdf.

11. "Fatherless Epidemic," National Center for Fathering, 2015, http://fathers.com/wp39/wp-content/uploads/2015/05/fatherlessInfographic.png.

12. "Fathering in America," National Center for Fathering, May 2009, 3, http://fathers.com/wp39/wp-content/uploads/2007/04/2009_Fathering_in_America_Summary.pdf.

13. CNN Library, "Mass Shootings in the US Fast Facts," CNN, accessed January 24, 2020, https://www.cnn.com/2019/08/19/us/mass-shootings-fast-facts/index.html.

14. W. Bradford Wilcox, "Sons of Divorce, School Shooters," December 16, 2013, https://www.aei.org/articles/sons-of-divorce-school-shooters/.

15. Paul Kengor, "Shootings and Fatherlessness: A Clarification on the Data," Crisis Magazine, March 9, 2018, https://www.crisismagazine.com/2018/fatherless-shooters-clarification-data.

16. Overview of John J. Smithbaker, *The Great American Rescue Mission: Reaching and Healing the Fatherless* (Dunham Books, 2018), accessed January 24, 2020, https://www.fathersinthefield.com/the-great-american-rescue-mission/.

17. Suzanne Venker, "Missing Fathers and America's Broken Boys—The Vast Majority of Mass Shooters Come From Broken Homes," FOX News, LLC, updated February 20, 2018, https://www.foxnews.com/opinion/missing-fathers-and-americas-broken-boys-the-vast-majority-of-mass-shooters-come-from-broken-homes.

18. Foreman with Davis, *Fatherhood by George*, 11–15.

19. Foreman with Davis, *Fatherhood by George*, 105–106.

20. Larry Stockstill, *Model Man: From Integrity to Legacy* (Shippensburg, PA: Destiny Image Publishers, 2015), 21, https://www.amazon.com/Model-Man-Integrity-Larry-Stockstill/dp/0768406838.

Chapter 12

1. Bruce Lowitt, "'Wrong Way' Riegels Takes Off Into History," *St. Petersburg Times*, September 26, 1999, https://web.archive.org/web/20160414122459/http://www.sptimes.com/News/92699/Sports/_Wrong_Way__Riegels_t.shtml.
2. Dave Newhouse, "An Infamous Rose Bowl, Cal v. Georgia Tech, 1929," Bear Insider, January 3, 2013, https://web.archive.org/web/20130410142031/http://www.bearinsider.com/news/story.php?article=356.
3. Wendy Wang, "Who Cheats More? The Demographics of Infidelity in America," Institute for Family Studies, January 10, 2018, https://ifstudies.org/blog/who-cheats-more-the-demographics-of-cheating-in-america.
4. "Infidelity Statistics," Divorce Source, May 29, 2015, https://www.divorcesource.com/blog/infidelity-statistics/.
5. Covenant Eyes, "Porn Stats," 2018, https://www.covenanteyes.com/pornstats/.
6. "Josephson Institute of Ethics Releases Study on High School Character and Adult Conduct," Josephson Institute of Ethics, press release, October 29, 2009, https://josephsoninstitute.org/surveys/.
7. Douglas T. Kenrick, "The 7 Worst Things About Being a Male," *Psychology Today*, January 29, 2012, https://www.psychologytoday.com/us/blog/sex-murder-and-the-meaning-life/201201/the-7-worst-things-about-being-male.
8. James Dobson, *Dads and Sons* (Carol Stream, IL: Tyndale Momentum, 2013), 39, https://books.google.com/books?id=vUt1AgAAQBAJ.
9. Mark 7:21–23, NKJV.
10. Justin Trudeau, "Why I'm Raising My Kids to Be Feminists," *Marie Claire*, October 11, 2017, https://www.marieclaire.com/politics/a12811748/justin-trudeau-raising-kids-feminist/.
11. Michael Ian Black, "The Boys Are Not All Right," *New York Times*, February 21, 2018, https://www.nytimes.com/2018/02/21/opinion/boys-violence-shootings-guns.html.
12. Allie Stuckey, "Make Men Masculine Again," PragerU video, August 5, 2018, https://www.prageru.com/video/make-men-masculine-again/.
13. John 15:5.

Chapter 13

1. 2 Samuel 20:1.
2. Blue Letter Bible, s.v. "*bĕliya'al*," accessed January 25, 2020, https://www.blueletterbible.org/lang/lexicon/lexicon.cfm?Strongs=H1100&t=ESV.
3. 2 Samuel 20:2, TLB, emphasis added.
4. Colossians 2:8.
5. Isaiah 30:15, NKJV.
6. 2 Kings 23:25.

Chapter 14

1. Dan Favale, "Michael Jordan's Unofficial Guide to Success in the NBA," Bleacher Report, February 14, 2013, https://bleacherreport.com/articles/1529861-michael-jordans-unofficial-guide-to-success-in-the-nba.
2. 1 Samuel 30:6.

3. Psalm 56, NKJV.
4. Psalm 27:10, KJV.
5. Psalm 50:15.
6. Romans 12:2.

Chapter 15

1. Stephen Mansfield, *Mansfield's Book of Manly Men: An Utterly Invigorating Guide to Being Your Most Masculine Self* (Nashville: Thomas Nelson, 2013), 18–19, https://books.google.com/books?id=HAJKgiJSRiMC&q.
2. Blue Letter Bible, s.v. "*Nĕchemyah*," accessed January 27, 2020, https://www.blueletterbible.org/lang/lexicon/lexicon.cfm?Strongs=H5166&t=ESV.
3. See Nehemiah 5.
4. Isaiah 44–45.
5. Ezra 1:2, NIV.
6. Proverbs 21:1, NKJV.
7. Ezra 1:4.
8. Nehemiah 9:20, NLT.

Chapter 16

1. Nehemiah 4:14.
2. Nehemiah 2:18, NKJV.
3. 2 Corinthians 10:4, NKJV.
4. Nehemiah 4:16–18, NIV.
5. Ephesians 6:10–11, 17.
6. Ephesians 6:12, NKJV.
7. Isaiah 54:17, NKJV; Romans 8:31.
8. Florence Nightingale, "A Woman's Vision of God," *Florence Nightingale's Theology: Essays, Letters and Journal Notes*, ed. Lynn McDonald (Waterloo, Ontario: Wilfrid Laurier University Press, 2002), 226–227, https://books.google.com/books?id=VcNoBNcV0XsC&q.
9. Proverbs 4:23, NIV.
10. 1 Corinthians 6:19.
11. Romans 8:11.
12. Nehemiah 3:1.

Chapter 17

1. Nehemiah 1:11.
2. Benjamin Reno Downer, "Cupbearer," in *The International Standard Bible Encyclopedia*, vol. 2, ed. James Orr (Chicago: The Howard-Severance Co., 1915), 766, https://books.google.com/books?id=wYIPAAAAYAAJ.
3. Nehemiah 1:3, NKJV.
4. Nehemiah 2:12.
5. Nehemiah 2:6–8.
6. Proverbs 21:1, NKJV.
7. Nehemiah 6:16, NKJV.

Chapter 18

1. 1 Samuel 8:7.
2. 1 Samuel 13:13–14, NKJV.
3. 1 Samuel 16:12–14.

4. 1 Samuel 22:2, NIV.
5. Bibleinfo, s.v. "remnant," accessed January 28, 2020, https://www.bibleinfo.com/en/topics/remnant.
6. Mike Porter, "God's Anointed: In a Cave, Surrounded by Misfits," *Mike's Place on the Web* (blog), September 22, 2009, https://witzend.wordpress.com/2009/09/22/gods-anointed-in-a-cave-surrounded-by-misfits/.
7. "Verse-by-Verse Bible Commentary: 1 Samuel 22:2," StudyLight.org, accessed January 28, 2020, https://www.studylight.org/commentary/1-samuel/22-2.html.
8. Porter, "God's Anointed."
9. Isaiah 5:20.
10. 1 Kings 19:10.
11. 1 Kings 19:18, NKJV.
12. Daniel 3.
13. Daniel 5–6.
14. Genesis 45:2.
15. Julie Clinton, *Becoming a Woman of Extraordinary Faith: What If You Gave It All to God?* (Eugene, OR: Harvest House, 2011), 79, https://books.google.com/books?id=usAf-KyD_JIC.
16. Genesis 45:24, NKJV.
17. Genesis 50:20, NKJV.
18. Bobby Bowden with Steve Ellis, *Bobby Bowden's Tales from the Seminole Sidelines* (Champaign, IL: Sports Publishing, 2004), 163–164, https://www.amazon.com/Bobby-Bowdens-Tales-Seminole-Sideline/dp/1582614067.
19. Bowden with Ellis, *Bobby Bowden's Tales from the Seminole Sidelines*, 164–165.
20. Steve Ellis and Bill Vilona, *Pure Gold: Bobby Bowden—An Inside Look* (Champaign, IL: Sports Publishing, 2006), 135–136, https://www.google.com/books/edition/Pure_Gold/_wDazqNu4iQC.
21. Pat Williams with Jim Denney, *The Difference You Make: Changing Your World through the Impact of Your Influence* (Grand Rapids, MI: Revell Books, 2013), 202, https://www.amazon.com/Difference-You-Make-Changing-Influence/dp/0800721683.

Chapter 19

1. 1 Samuel 17:45–47, MSG.
2. Thomas Hauser, *Muhammad Ali: His Life and Times* (New York: Simon and Schuster, 1991), 61, https://www.amazon.com/Muhammad-Ali-His-Life-Times/dp/0671779710/ref=sr_1_1?crid=25PPQ8JLG6VJE.
3. John 2:15–17, NKJV.
4. This section was adapted from Tim Clinton and Mark Laaser, *The Fight of Your Life: Manning Up to the Challenge of Sexual Integrity* (Shippensburg, PA: Destiny Image, 2016). Used by permission.
5. Sam Childers, *Another Man's War: The True Story of One Man's Battle to Save Children in the Sudan* (Nashville: Thomas Nelson, 2009), 30.
6. "Crisis in Sudan," US Committee for Refugees, April 2001, https://web.archive.org/web/20041210024759/http://www.refugees.org/news/crisis/sudan.htm.
7. Childers, *Another Man's War*, back cover.
8. Matthew 10:28.
9. Mark 8:36, NKJV.

Chapter 20

1. 1 Samuel 16:12, NLT.
2. 1 Samuel 17:24, NKJV.
3. 1 Samuel 17:25.
4. 1 Samuel 17:26, NKJV.
5. 1 Timothy 4:12, NKJV.
6. 1 Samuel 17:28, NKJV.
7. See 1 Samuel 17:32.
8. 1 Samuel 17:34–37, NKJV.
9. Heather Pringle, "Ancient Slingshot Was as Deadly as a .44 Magnum," National Geographic, May 24, 2017, https://www.nationalgeographic.com/news/2017/05/ancient-slingshot-lethal-44-magnum-scotland/.
10. 1 Samuel 17:39.
11. 1 Samuel 17:40.
12. 1 Samuel 17:42–44.
13. 1 Samuel 17:51–53.

Chapter 21

1. "Hall of Fame Feature: Robert Brunet," Louisiana Tech University, October 19, 2015, https://latechsports.com/news/2015/10/19/Hall_of_Fame_Feature_Robert_Brunet.aspx.
2. "Hall of Fame Feature," Louisiana Tech University.
3. "Hall of Fame Feature," Louisiana Tech University.
4. 1 Corinthians 16:9, NKJV.
5. 1 Samuel 17:45, 47.
6. See Exodus 2:11–3:22.
7. Martin Luther King Jr., "Why Jesus Called a Man a Fool," sermon, Mount Pisgah Missionary Baptist Church, August 27, 1967, https://kinginstitute.stanford.edu/king-papers/documents/why-jesus-called-man-fool-sermon-delivered-mount-pisgah-missionary-baptist.

Chapter 22

1. 2 Samuel 23:15.
2. 2 Samuel 23:17, NKJV.
3. 1 Chronicles 11:17–19.
4. Linda Robertson, "Aaron Feis Lauded as a Hero for Shielding Students From Bullets," *Miami Herald*, February 19, 2018, https://www.miamiherald.com/news/local/community/broward/article200965774.html.
5. Emily Shapiro, "Slain Football Coach Ran 'Toward Danger' to Save Students in School Shooting, Sheriff Says at Funeral," ABC News, February 22, 2018, https://abcnews.go.com/beta-story-container/US/funeral-held-today-football-coach-killed-protecting-students/story?id=53272195.
6. Robertson, "Aaron Feis Lauded as a Hero for Shielding Students From Bullets."
7. John 15:13.
8. Johnathan Fontenot, "The Christian Police Officer," Thibodaux PD Officer Blog, April 30, 2013, https://thibodauxpd.wordpress.com/2013/04/30/the-christian-police-officer-by-officer-johnathan-fontenot/.
9. Matthew 16:25, PHILLIPS.
10. John 3:16.
11. 1 Corinthians 16:13–14, NKJV.

Chapter 23

1. See Numbers 12:3, NKJV.
2. Luke 9:28–31.
3. 1 Kings 19:4.
4. James 2:23, NKJV.
5. Psalm 130:3–4.
6. Judges 15:14.
7. Judges 14:19, NKJV.
8. Judges 13:5.
9. Judges 16:17.
10. Proverbs 6:24–28, NKJV.
11. Proverbs 9:17–18, NKJV.
12. Judges 16:20.
13. Proverbs 5:20.
14. Judges 16:28.
15. Judges 16:30.
16. Romans 5:20, NKJV.
17. David Wilkerson, *Have You Felt Like Giving Up Lately?: A Source Book for Healing Your Hurts* (Grand Rapids, MI: Revell, 1980), 84, 89.
18. Matthew 26:74, NKJV.
19. John 21:15–17.
20. Matthew 1:1.
21. Psalm 32:3–4.
22. James 1:14–15, NKJV.
23. Psalm 51:1–11, NKJV.
24. 2 Samuel 12:20.
25. 2 Samuel 12:23.
26. Edwin Louis Cole, *Maximized Manhood: A Guide to Family Survival* (New Kensington, PA: Whitaker House, 2000), 72, https://www.amazon.com/Maximized-Manhood-Guide-Family-Survival/dp/0883686554.

Chapter 24

1. John 19:5.
2. "Singular 'They,'" *Merriam-Webster*, updated September 2019, https://www.merriam-webster.com/words-at-play/singular-nonbinary-they.
3. Henry George Liddell and Robert Scott, *A Greek-English Lexicon*, s.v. "τέκτων," accessed January 29, 2020, http://www.perseus.tufts.edu/hopper/text?doc=Perseus%3Atext%3A1999.04.0057%3Aentry%3Dte%2Fktwn.
4. R. T. Kendall, *Holy Fire: A Balanced, Biblical Look at the Holy Spirit's Work in Our Lives* (Lake Mary, FL: Charisma House, 2014), 16, https://books.google.com/books?id=OeTrAQAAQBAJ&dqs.
5. Jerry Boykin and Stu Weber, *The Warrior Soul: Five Powerful Principles to Make You a Stronger Man of God* (Lake Mary, FL: Charisma House, 2015), 71, 73, 191, https://books.google.com/books?id=7v9WBQAAQBAJ&q.
6. Galatians 2:20.
7. Galatians 4:19.
8. Edwin Louis Cole, foreword in *Men Mentoring Men: A Men's Discipleship Course*, Daryl G. Donovan (Lima, OH: CSS Publishing, 1998), 5, https://books.google.com/books?id=eOiRGPzN61sC&pg.
9. 1 Timothy 5:8.

Chapter 25

1. Romans 1:20, NLV.
2. Charles E. Hummel, *Tyranny of the Urgent*, reprint (Downers Grove, IL: InterVarsity Press, 1967), http://www.discipleshiplibrary.com/pdfs/ED0004.pdf.
3. Hummel, *Tyranny of the Urgent*.
4. James 4:14.
5. Psalm 90:12, NKJV.
6. Acts 13:36.

My **FREE GIFT** to You

I'm so happy you read this book. It's so important to reclaim the true meaning of biblical masculinity — especially today.

As my way of saying thank you, I am offering you a few gifts:

- **PDF Download: Printable Poster**

- **E-book:** *Take It Back*

- **Video Download:** *Take It Back* **from Ignite**

- **Audio Download:** *What It Means to Be a Godly Man*

- **PDF Download:** *Boys to Men*

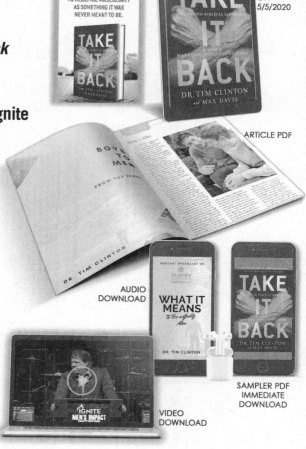

To get this **FREE GIFT**, please go to:

TimClintonBooks.com/gift

Thanks again and God bless you,

Tim Clinton